THE
NEWFOUNDLAND
GENTLE GIANT

JoAnn Riley

ILLUSTRATIONS BY ALAN RILEY

Alpine
Blue Ribbon Books
Loveland, Colorado

The Newfoundland, Gentle Giant

Copyright 2004, by JoAnn Riley

Copyright 1985, *The Newfoundland*, by Betty McDonnell and JoAnn Riley

Library of Congress Cataloging-in-Publication Data

Riley, JoAnn.
      The Newfoundland, gentle giant / JoAnn Riley ; illustrations by Alan Riley.
            p. cm.
      Includes bibliographical references and index.
      ISBN 1-57779-061-8
      1. Newfoundland dog. I. Title

SF429.N4.R552 2004
636.73--dc22

                                        2004045083

The information contained in this book is complete and accurate to the best of our knowledge. All recommendations are made without guarantee on the part of the author or Alpine Publications, Inc. The author and publisher disclaim any liability with the use of this information.

This book is available at special quantity discounts for breeders and for club promotions, premiums, or educational use. Write for details.

For the sake of simplicity, the terms "he" or "she" are sometimes used to identify an animal or person. These are used in the generic sense only. No discrimination of any kind is intended toward either sex.

Captions list the full name of the dog(s) pictured with the kennel name in italic. Kennel names denote where the dog was bred. For the names of the breeders, refer to the list of kennels in Appendix A. If there are two or more breeders or owners, their names are listed as part of the caption.

Many manufacturers secure trademark rights for their products. When Alpine Publications is aware of a trademark claim, we identify the product name by using initial capital letters.

Cover Design: Laura Newport
Cover Photo: Norwegian, Swedish CH Bikorella's Oula, bred and owned by Astrid Indreboe and Knut Gjersem. Photo by Astrid Indreboe.
Back Cover Photos: (left) Soren Wesseltoft, (right) JoAnn Riley.
Editing: Lisa McGinley and B. J. McKinney
Layout: Laura Newport
Illustrations: Alan Riley unless otherwise indicated

First printing April 2004

3 4 5 6 7 8 9 0

Printed in the United States of America

CONTENTS

Chapter One: MEET THE NEWFOUNDLAND

    • Disadvantages • Advantages • Newfoundland Character • Summary

Chapter Two: HISTORY AND FUNCTION

Chapter Three: THE BREED STANDARD

    • Official AKC Newfoundland Standard • The Kennel Club
        (Great Britain) Standard for the Newfoundland

Chapter Four: CHOOSING YOUR NEWFOUNDLAND

Chapter Five: YOUR NEW PUPPY

    • Helping Your Puppy Adjust • Puppy Proofing Your Home • Training and Playing with Puppy
        • Leash Training • Housebreaking • Feeding • Exercise and Conditioning
            • Routine Health Care • Grooming • Summary

Chapter Six: CARING FOR THE ADULT NEWFOUNDLAND

    • Diet • Bloat • Eating Problems • Shelter and Protection • Traveling with Your Newf
        • Health Care • Orthopedic Problems • External Parasites • Internal Parasites

Chapter Seven: GROOMING YOUR NEWFOUNDLAND

    • Brushing and Trimming • Bathing • Trimming Nails • Other Routine Grooming

This book is gratefully dedicated to my husband, Alan,
without whose help, my experience in the dog world would have been
greatly limited. He encouraged me to participate in,
and often shared in, activities outside his own interests.
His experiences in training and in hiking with our dogs brought
to both of us a new dimension (dogs as partners in the wilderness.)

ABOUT THE AUTHOR

JoAnn Riley grew up without the thing she most wanted—a dog. After five years of marriage, Alan and JoAnn were ready to move out of their apartment and into their first house. Unable to wait any longer, they bought a Boxer puppy the day JoAnn left her job, just before the move.

After leaving Minneapolis for Seattle five years later, the Rileys made a long research of large and giant breeds as the right companion for their Boxer (and for themselves). Neither had ever seen a live Newfoundland, but from pictures and reading about the breed's sweet character, they decided on this breed. There were no breeders in the area, so they ordered their first Newf by telephone. When the puppy, Golly, came out of his crate at the airport, he became the first Newf they had ever laid eyes on. That was in 1963 and they have had Newfoundlands ever since.

Both JoAnn and Alan have been deeply involved with the breed. Their first interest has always been the joy of living with Newfs. Their second interest has been the pleasure of engaging in activities with their dogs. JoAnn has been active mostly in shows, first as an exhibitor, and later as a judge. Alan's interest revolved around his love of hiking in the mountains of Washington and neighboring states. It was natural that the Newfs became his companions, and sometimes his protectors. Both JoAnn and Alan supported each other's interests, and together they have shared a full life with the wonderful Newfoundland Dog.

The Rileys are honorary members of the Newfoundland Club of America, where JoAnn has served in many capacities through the years. She chaired the Standard and Illustrated Guide Committees. She was the first Chairman of the NCA Judges Education Committee. She was also one of the first Newfoundland Club of America Water Test judges.

JoAnn began judging in 1976, when she judged bitches at the National Specialty. Since then she has judged dogs at the 1980 National, intersex at the 1986 National, and both the veteran sweepstakes and the maturity class at the 2002 National. She has also judged in several European countries, as well as Australia and New Zealand. JoAnn is currently approved by the American Kennel Club to judge most of the Working Group in the USA, and has judged some of those breeds abroad as well.

The Newfoundland, gentle giant. Miss Maya walks quietly on lead with young Laura. Photo © Soren Wesseltoft.

FOREWORD

It is with great pleasure that I am able to recommend the newest Newfoundland book to your bookshelf. Author JoAnn Riley brings forty years of experience in the breed. She and her artist husband, Alan, have bred and exhibited their Seamount Newfoundlands in the Pacific Northwest since 1963.

With her international overview of the breed Mrs. Riley has the larger picture of the breed. She is prejudiced only in preferring dogs that meet the breed standard. Having worked with her dogs, I know that she appreciates the true Newfoundland temperament that makes this breed so unique. In 1985 JoAnn and I co-authored *The Newfoundland* and *The Newfoundland Handbook,* published by Denlinger Publishing. In this new book she has solicited photos of Newfoundlands from around the world. Breeders graciously responded to her request for both show and candid photos. You will enjoy meeting the newest sampling of elite Newfoundlands, and you will enjoy the timeless drawings of Newfoundlands by Alan Riley.

A number of changes have occurred in the breed in the last twenty years. Consistency is desirable in any breed and there appears to be greater consistency among Newfoundlands than ten or twelve years ago, especially among dogs found in the show ring. These are the dogs that are, or will be, the progenitors of future generations.

There is a greater emphasis today on the working abilities of Newfoundlands, and wider participation in working activities by Newf owners and breeders. This helps insure that these inborn characteristics will be preserved for the future of the breed. Both the AKC and the Newfoundland Club of America have added to the trials and activities for dogs and their owners to preserve the dogs' abilities to do their traditional tasks.

Research and advances in veterinary medicine have made it possible to improve health, not only through new or more effective treatments, but by better diagnostics and preventive medicine. Diagnostic screening and registries for dogs clear of certain hereditary or congenital problems help make it possible for breeders to avoid breeding animals with these problems. It also allows buyers to choose puppies from litters of parents "cleared" for the problems. At present, only the manifestation of the problem can be screened for, but genome mapping may make it possible to declare a dog genetically free of a disease.

Environmentalists and lovers of the outdoors, the Rileys wrote the still popular book *Taking Your Dog Backpacking* in 1979. After the book was out of print, the rights were purchased by the Newfoundland Club of America. Alan donated an additional chapter to update the book, along with illustrations.

Betty McDonnell
Newfoundland breeder, exhibitor, and judge
Past president of the Newfoundland Club of America
Current chair of the Judges' Education Committee
Honorary Member of the Newfoundland Club of America

ACKNOWLEGEMENTS

This book would not be complete without acknowledging Betty McDonnell's contribution. The material in the former book (which we co-authored) provided the framework for this book, which includes both new written material and pictures. But much of Betty's philosophy has been retained.

I want to thank all of those who contributed the photographs. They were willing to loan their cherished pictures of beloved dogs, trusting them to the mail, to me, and to the publishers for safekeeping. I would especially like to recognize Soren Wesseltoft, a Newfoundland breeder and professional photographer in Denmark, who was most generous in sharing his outstanding work.

Joringle Seaside, bred by Inge and Bent Hegnsvang (Denmark) and owned by Eva Obojes (Austria). Photo by Arno Froehlich.

MEET THE NEWFOUNDLAND

Is This the Dog for You?

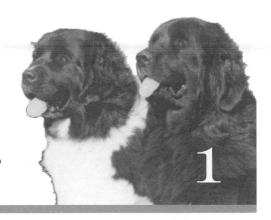

The Newfoundland breed is blessed with traits that make these dogs delightful and fascinating companions. A casual encounter reveals a Newfoundland's warmth of character. Living with a Newfoundland reveals his generosity, his wisdom, and his exceptional ability to communicate. However, being charmed by a Newf at a park or seeing one in a movie or television program, is not a good reason to decide you "have to have" a Newfie. Unfortunately, this is how some dog owners make their decision to own a certain breed. No dog or breed should be chosen based upon such limited exposure. While an appealing appearance is a consideration in choosing a breed, the appearance of any given dog is not necessarily how the breed looks as a whole. How any given dog behaves on the screen, especially an actor dog, is a poor indication of actual behavior. Before considering a Newfoundland (or any breed) for a pet, it is important to study the breed by talking with owners and breeders, visiting kennels, and reading about the breed. Be aware that dogs seen at shows are expertly groomed and produced by knowledgeable breeders who are showing their best dogs. If you buy a dog from someone who bred his or her pet bitch to whatever male could be found, you are not likely to end up with a dog that looks like the ones you saw at a dog show.

The Newfoundland is recognized as a gentle, benevolent, sweet dog. There are few accounts of the Newfoundland that do not

include such words. These characteristics, combined with an impressive size, make the Newfoundland, or "Newf," as he is affectionately called, a most appealing creature. With a broad skull and muzzle, "chunky cheeks," and wide-set eyes, he maintains an almost baby-like expression that seems universally appealing in a biological sense. In addition, a

Ch. *Cayuga's* When You Are Smiling, owned by Winnie and Soren Wesseltoft. This bitch was bred in Italy and is owned in Denmark. Photo by Soren Wesseltoft.

overall bear-like appearance adds to his charm; he is the teddy bear of one's childhood come to life.

Male Newfoundlands, in general, are heavier and taller than bitches. Adult Newfoundlands generally range in weight between 110 and 160 pounds. Height ranges from 24 to 32 inches at the shoulder, with the average being 28 inches for dogs and 26 inches for bitches. However, extremes of both height and weight occur in either direction from the ideal in both sexes.

The Newfoundland is a double-coated breed, with a moderately long, coarse outer coat and a soft, dense undercoat. Weekly grooming is almost essential. During warm weather or when a bitch comes in season, the Newf will shed copious amounts of undercoat which must be brushed frequently to prevent matting.

Black, or white with black, are the most common coat colors, but Newfs also come in brown, gray, and black with white. White markings are acceptable on black, brown, and gray dogs (see the chapter on the Newfoundland Standard for an exact description of acceptable markings).

Any heavy-coated breed prefers a cool climate, but Newfs can adapt to heat. They tend to permanently shed the insulating undercoat in hot climates. The coat of black dogs will absorb the sun's heat very quickly, making both shade and cool drinking water essential in hot weather.

The Newfoundland is an active, working dog that needs daily exercise. Even with a large yard to move around in, many Newfs choose to be couch potatoes. It is up to the owner to see that they get exercise needed to maintain health. Walking with your dog is good both for him and for you. Playing with your dog, training, and swimming all provide exercise. Newfs, and indeed most mammals, tend to be less active in hot weather. However, under most conditions, this agreeable dog will be active or inactive according to his owner's pleasure. The owner, in turn, is responsible for seeing that the dog gets exercise appropriate to the weather as well as the dog's age and condition.

Along with his agreeable nature, the Newf is probably best known for his swimming ability. His webbed feet, broad chest, and well-sprung ribs make him a natural

The body lies almost parallel to the water as "Sunny" swims in a pool. Breeder/owners Denise and Marc Castonguay. Photo by Kendall DeMenech.

Newfs love to be with people and these dogs were welcome guests at a Danish wedding. Photo by Birgitta Gothen.

swimmer, and his oily double coat effectively repels water. The Newfoundland does not dog-paddle, but swims with long strokes. His body lies almost parallel to the surface of the water as he swims, with his hindquarters only slightly lower in the water than his forequarters. Even though they hold their heads above water, many Newfs, especially when swimming at leisure, gulp water as they move along. Others squeak or whine, apparently in pleasure, for this is a trait of some of the most enthusiastic Newfoundland swimmers.

Some Newfs have a stronger desire to swim than do others. Often this is the result of early exposure to water. Young puppies usually will enter water and begin swimming with little or no encouragement. A dog introduced to water at an older age may require coaxing and encouragement. Sometimes these late starters become the greatest enthusiasts.

One bitch, not exposed to water until she was taken on a camping trip at the age of nine months, refused to swim even though her male companion took every opportunity to cool himself in the frigid mountain rivers. The bitch would wade in but would not swim, even when sticks were thrown for the dogs to retrieve—a favorite sport on land. On the trip home, the heat was intense. When her owners found a lake with a temperature tolerable to humans, they plunged in, accompanied by the male Newf. This was too much for the bitch. Perhaps she couldn't stand being left out, or feared for her owners' safety. In any event, she jumped in, swam out to her owners, and circled them repeatedly. Eventually this bitch became an outstanding swimmer that loved the water.

The circling behavior is typical of Newfoundlands when swimming with humans. It appears to be a protective response born of a natural instinct for water rescue. It is curious that an animal so at home in the water should recognize the vulnerability of humans in this element and fear for their safety.

It is a common experience for parents of young children to see their Newfs station themselves between the children and deeper water. Some Newfs try to herd swimming children from the water, or

Ch. *Pouch Cove's* Say Your Prayers, a male Newf, with a puppy. This patience with young things is typical of the Newfoundland breed. Owner and photographer, Mary Jane Spackman.

hover closely as self-appointed life-guards. Adult swimmers complain that their activities are hampered by their anxious Newfs, who insist upon circling or staying close.

A *Midnight Lady* puppy. Puppy fuzz makes baby Newfs seem like stuffed toys…too adorable to be real. Owned by V. Javorck. Photo by Atilla Soos.

Newfies have a great need for human attention. Although Newfoundlands can be kept successfully as kennel dogs with other dog companions, each Newf needs human contact, attention, and, ideally, some work or training on a regular basis. A Newf can be kept as an outdoor dog in a fenced yard with room to explore and exercise, provided he also gets individual attention and training. Another dog companion is ideal when owners are gone all day. No dog should be chained or allowed to run loose. Probably the most content Newfs are those that live with their owners as house pets. They are stimulated by the coming and going of family and guests, being talked to and petted frequently, and, above all, being with the people they love. Being left alone without regular attention is unfair to the dog.

DISADVANTAGES

It is especially important to be aware of the negatives as well as the positives of owning any breed of dog. While large size can be appealing, it has its disadvantages. The Newf's long, wagging tail can sweep all but the heaviest objects from low tables and counters. Having a Newf around is a bit like having a toddler in the house; it is necessary to remove items that may be broken or damaged from within reach of little hands (and long tails).

Since animals are, by nature, opportunists in the matter of finding food, the size of a Newf makes it easy for him to help himself to food items a smaller dog could not reach. Even food placed at the rear of a kitchen counter may be within reach of a very large, determined dog if he stands up with his front paws on the counter. In the wild, any food not being defended by another creature is fair game. It is expecting a lot to assume a pet dog thinks any differently. Some dogs seem to understand, intrinsically, what is off limits to them. Others can be trained to avoid temptation. Then there are those that simply cannot resist the lure of food. For them, it is up to the owner to keep temptation out of the dog's way. It is possible to train a dog to accept food only from his feeding dish or from his owner's hands, but this has its disadvantages if the dog must be kenneled or must stay overnight at the vet's. It is best to train yourself to avoid leaving temptation within easy reach of the dog. That includes remembering to pick up the party dip from the coffee table after the guests leave.

It is essential to train a large breed puppy not to jump or stand up against humans. Children and the elderly, especially, cannot defend themselves against such onslaughts, however friendly and well-intended. Most guests or people encountered during walks, regardless of their size and physical competence, will not take kindly to such overtures.

Newf puppies grow rapidly and one must be careful not to overstress their

Denise Castonguay, breeder and owner of Am. Can. Int'l Ch. *CastaNewf's* So To Speak, welcomes a warm greeting from "Sunny." Her well-trained dogs would not do this unless invited. Photo by Pam Mohr.

joints nor to over-supplement them during the growing stage. Like most fast-growing large breeds of dogs, Newfoundlands are candidates for joint and bone problems such as hip dysplasia, elbow dysplasia, and rupture of the cruciate ligament. When selecting a dog, be sure that any dog over two years of age has been x-rayed for hip dysplasia, or that the parents of any puppy you are considering have been certified free of the disease by the Orthopedic Foundation for Animals (OFA). Never let a child ride on the back of your Newfoundland, and

Kilykas Castlepine Jamielee might not be welcome in the house immediately after her dip in the river. Jamie is owned by Zoe Montague. Photo by Robert Carpenter.

discourage puppies from jumping until they are at least a year old.

Another consideration is transportation. Transporting a large dog requires a large vehicle, especially if the dog is to be carried in a crate. Crates are the safest way to transport a dog in the car, but the giant-size crate required by this breed is a costly investment. However, a good airline or wire crate will last the lifetime of a dog or longer.

The costs of maintaining any dog over his lifetime far exceed the purchase price of the dog. Newfies, like most large breeds, are not inexpensive to buy and maintain. Feeding costs are quite reasonable, but supplies, equipment, boarding and veterinary fees are higher than for small breeds. Maintenance costs and unforeseen expenses should be included in the budget when planning to add a Newf to the family.

As a housedog, the Newf has certain disadvantages. He will carry into the house—on coat, mouth, and feet—dust, rain, mud, and outdoor debris such as grass clippings and leaves. Newfoundlands also shed profusely at times, and some drool. They are sloppy eaters and drinkers.

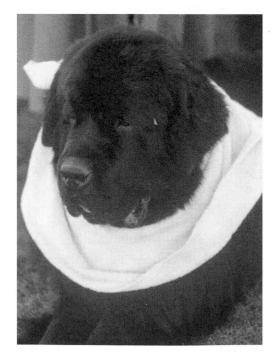

Expect your Newf to drool, especially when nervous. This dog waits his turn at ringside with a "slobber towel" around his neck to keep him clean. Photo © Judith Strom.

Newfs love children and are very protective of them. Ch. *Bjornebanden's* Miss Maya del Castelbarco shows typical Newf patience with Laura. Owned by breeders. Photo by Soren Wesseltoft.

Puppies may paddle in their water bowls or drink with one foot in the bowl. Most of these annoyances can be dealt with, but a Newf is not for the fastidious housekeeper, nor for one whose clothes must be immaculate at all times.

If you want a Newf, you need to accept the idea that your dog will have a wet mouth to some degree. Not all Newfs are heavy droolers. Some have wet mouths only after drinking or exercising, or when they become excited. Others slobber frequently. It is almost impossible to determine this when choosing a puppy, because puppies do not drool. It is not until a dog is nine months or older that this phenomenon begins. Being prepared takes some of the sting out of the experience. Plan to keep a "slobber towel" by the outside door so you can wipe your dog's mouth as soon as he comes inside. Keep another towel by the chair where you sit to read or watch TV so it will be handy if the dog comes to put his head in your lap (right after taking a drink from his water bowl)! Take a towel with you in the car so you can wipe your Newf if he gets hot or excited. You will do your vet a favor if you take a towel into the clinic with you. Most dogs get nervous at a veterinary clinic and this will bring on the drools. This may all sound formidable. If you think you cannot deal with it, don't get a Newf.

Long dog hairs on clothes, bare floors, carpets, and furniture are also part of living with a Newf. Your vacuum will take care of the carpets and a dust mop will take care of the floors. Clothes and furniture are readily brushed free of hair using a damp sponge. Sponge rubber seems to work better than a coarse kitchen sponge. If you wring it out well before using it on your

Newfoundland essentials—human companionship and water in which to cool off. Photo from The Newfoundland, © Stephenie Koplin.

clothes, the sponge will not leave damp spots on the fabric.

ADVANTAGES

While the disadvantages of a Newf as house dog are mere annoyances, the advantages are invaluable. You need never come home to an empty house. There is nothing like the unabashed joy of a Newf's greeting to lift your spirits as well as offer assurance that all is well. A dog is never judgmental. He offers love and trust in the worst of times as well as in the best.

The Newf is as amiable to live with as he appears upon first acquaintance. Newfs love people and thrive on human companionship. A Newf will not obviously attach himself to a single member of the family. If he has a preference, he still responds to others with warmth and affection. This quality makes the Newf a highly adaptable breed. Puppies and adult dogs usually adjust easily to loving, new homes.

The most endearing traits of this breed are sweetness, warmth, and good cheer. These dogs like to be close to their humans. Many Newfs are "leaners." If talked to in an obvious "dog talk" tone, they will lean into you. When you first come home and pet them in greeting, they will lean. If given a hug, they will lean. Newfs also love to follow anyone working outside. If the work is in one place, the dog will sit or lie down, often with his muzzle as close as possible to what is going on, as if everything is too interesting to miss. If the work

Newfs usually get along well with other dogs and animals. This *Bjornebanden* puppy and the lamb seem to be equally curious about each other. Puppy bred and owned by Winnie and Soren Wesseltoft. Photo by Soren Wesseltoft.

Nakiska's Judge Willoughby with Tucker, a Labrador puppy. Willy was bred by Ingrid and Chris Lyden and is owned by the author. Photo by author.

requires moving from place to place, the dog will follow.

Certain behaviors that are both amusing and endearing are common among many Newfs. "Lead carrying" is quite typical. After the lead has been attached, the dog will tip his head, grasp the lead in his mouth and proudly trot off with it. A charming characteristic is when a Newf's ears go back and down in response to a gesture or voice as if to say, "I saw what you did and I know it was for my benefit." I think of it as a Newfie "smile."

Some Newfs have a sense of humor and will respond to silly movements and faces made for their benefit. Others will find ways to tease or invite you to play. We had one Newf who would "steal" the hat off my husband's head at any opportunity, then run off, looking back to invite a chase. It is not uncommon to find a Newf sleeping in the bathtub. How they discover that the tub is a cool place to lie is puzzling, but it is certainly not an unusual habit.

Although the Newfoundland is not considered a guard dog, he does have a

Even though this older puppy has the child's hand in his mouth, he is obviously not biting down. Like the retrieving breeds, most Newfs are "soft-mouthed." Photo by Jan Boggio.

NEWFOUNDLAND CHARACTER

The following experiences of Newfoundlands and Newf owners can better describe the character of the Newfoundland than any labels we might attach to him.

Newfoundland lore abounds with tales of heroism, some documented, and others apocryphal. Probably the most noted account of a Newf rescue occurred in 1919. The steamer *Ethie* was flung against rocks during a storm along the coast of Nova Scotia. She began breaking up in the heavy swells. The lifeboats were washed away and one sailor was drowned in an attempt to reach shore with a line. As a last resort after boats from shore failed to reach the vessel, the ship's Newfoundland was sent overboard. The dog, Tang, struggled ashore with a line in his mouth. This made possible the rigging of a boatswain's chair by which all passengers and crew were rescued. Lloyds of London awarded Tang a medal for his deed.

Humanity is enriched by the selflessness of heroic deeds. There is something especially touching about canine heroism when creatures, which we tend to view as dependent and somewhat childlike, demonstrate intelligence, creativity, and generosity beyond our expectations.

Many years ago we were commonly asked if our Newfoundlands were black Saint Bernards. We encountered an older woman who identified our dog as a Newf. As we expressed pleasure and surprise at her recognition, she told us that she owed her life to a Newfoundland. Pressed for details, she told us that she was very young when the rescue occurred but she knew the story well because it had been told over and over within her family. She went on to explain that her family had made a trip by train from their home in Wisconsin to St. Paul, Minnesota, to buy a Newf puppy from a pet store. The puppy grew up with the children

strong protective instinct. If a family is asleep or away from home, the Newf acts as protector of the household. His deep bark alone will deter all but the most determined intruders. Newfs are not idle barkers. They do not bark out of boredom, and when they do sound off they sense a reason—an unusual sound, a ringing doorbell, or an unrecognized vehicle pulling into the driveway. Overall, they are a quiet breed. One dog lived to age thirteen and barked only twice, that we know of, in all those years.

A Newf is friendly toward guests, but when the door is opened to a stranger, a Newf can sense the "Who are you and what do you want?" attitude of his owner. He remains aloof until the owner's demeanor indicates trust. Even then, he may sense that something is not right. If a Newf does not relax his aloof stance after the owner indicates acceptance of a stranger, there is reason to rely on his doubt.

and usually accompanied them in their play activities. One day the children and their Newf went to play by a millpond near their rural home. The older children soon moved on to other activities while the girl and her younger brother stayed at the pond tossing sticks. Somehow both children tumbled into the water. The deep pond, with its steep sides, made it impossible for them to climb out, and they began to shout. The Newfoundland, who had gone with the older group, heard the shouts, raced back to the pond, dived in, and supported the girl until her brothers and sisters arrived to pull her out. In the meantime, the younger brother had slipped under the water. While one of the older children ran for help, the dog began diving for the boy. Even after a boat was brought in to drag the pond, the Newf continued to dive until the boy was pulled out, drowned. As a result of the prolonged diving, the dog developed an ear infection. Today he might have been saved but, given the treatment available at that time, the condition could not be cleared up and the dog had to be put to sleep.

When the youngsters in this boat, about a hundred yards from shore, called to Katrinka Too Much as if they were in distress, she dived from the dock and swam to them. They threw her the painter and she towed the boat to shore. Trinka had never dived or towed before. She was bred and owned by the author.

SUMMARY

Overall, the Newfoundland is a wonderful breed. Like any breed, Newfs have their drawbacks. You must take these into account before you decide on a Newfoundland so that you will be prepared to cope with and accept them as part of owning a very special dog. Evaluate your commitment to owning a dog. If there is any doubt in your mind about being willing to meet his needs, opt for a less demanding pet.

The Tibetan Mastiff may be a progenitor of the Newfoundland. Shown here is a contemporary Tibetan Mastiff, World and multi-champion *Himalaya's* Emir Pasha, bred by S. Ochsenbein and owned by Martha Feltenstein. Photo by Jeff Kaiser.

HISTORY AND FUNCTION

HOW NEWFOUNDLANDS CAME TO BE

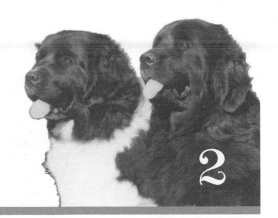

2

THERE SEEMS TO BE NO FAVORED THEORY ON the origin of the Newfoundland dog, but most authorities agree that the breed originated on the large island province in eastern Canada that gave it its name. In the United States, the dog is usually called a New´-fund-lund, with the accent on the first syllable. Canadians pronounce it as New-fund-land´ with the accent on the last syllable. Theirs is, no doubt, the more correct pronunciation since the dog is named for one of their provinces.

The Newfoundland is neither an ancient breed, such as the Saluki, of which there are pictorial records dating back seven thousand years, nor is it a fairly recently-created breed such as the Doberman Pinscher, which dates from about 1890. One theory of the Newfoundland's origin holds that the Norsemen in their early explorations brought large bear-like dogs, descended from the Tibetan Mastiff, to the Eastern shores of the New World. Another theory suggests that the Newf is a descendant of Tibetan Mastiffs that crossed the Bering Strait land bridge from Asia to North America. A third theory proposes that the Newf was a result of interbreeding among a native dog or dogs and the Great Pyrenees dogs brought to America by Basque fishermen. Both

Tibetan Mastiffs and Great Pyrenees are rather puzzling possibilities as progenitors because of the difference in temperament of these breeds, as compared to the Newfoundland. While the Newf has a warm, outgoing temperament, both the Tibetan Mastiff and the Great Pyrenees have a strong guarding instinct and are cool to strangers.

Over centuries, and even within centuries, breeders have changed certain characteristics of their various breeds, so that many dogs that appear in old illustrations are barely comparable to their contemporary

Quebec

Labrador

Newfoundland

An old etching of the Tibetan Mastiff. This breed is currently bred in the United States and now looks more like today's Newfs than the dog in the picture.

counterparts. The present Newf resembles pictures of the old Tibetan Mastiff more than it does many of the early Newfoundland specimens identified in illustrations.

The question of origin also involves whether the black dogs and the white with black dogs were originally two different breeds. Some owners of black and white Newfoundlands maintain that their dogs have specific character traits that are different from those of the black dogs. Whether this lends credence to the theory that they evolved from different breeds is difficult to assess, because both color types have been interbred for many years.

References to what appears to be a Newfoundland date back to the early 1600s, but the breed was not named until about 1775 when a George Cartwright referred to his own dog as a Newfoundland. A few years later, an English naturalist by the name of Bewick gave a description of an English Newfoundland, along with its measurements and an illustration. The picture showed a black and white dog of the type sometimes referred to as the Landseer Newfoundland.

Despite a lack of evidence to support a single theory of origin, there is no lack of information concerning the breed's existence since Bewick's time. Historical records, art, and literature document the Newfoundland's past.

Although the Newfoundland originated in North America, the breed prospered in England. During the late 1700s, a law was passed in Newfoundland forbidding ownership of more than one family dog. The Newf population on the island diminished, and it was not until the early 1900s that the breed was revived in its homeland through the efforts of the Honorable Harold MacPherson at his Westerland Kennels.

Meanwhile, in England the breed perpetuated and, with selective breeding, became recognized as purebred. About the turn of the century the breed began to flourish, becoming a favorite pet and children's companion. Sentimental pictures from the Victorian era often show a child with a Newfoundland dog.

The foundation of today's Standard for the breed traces back to the dog Siki, of the

The late Kitty Drury, co founder of *Dryad* Kennels, awarding a ribbon at a dog show in 1970. Photo by Bennett Assoc.

type established in England. Three Siki sons were imported into the United States. Ch. Harlingen Neptune and Ch. Seafarer, Siki sons owned by Elizabeth Loring Power of Waseeka Kennels, were dominant show winners of their time. They and their get became the foundation stock for the type found in present-day dogs.

Also considered foundation kennels were the Coastwise Kennels of Beatrice and Major Godsol and the Dryad Kennels of Maynard and Kitty Drury. These breeders produced dogs of excellent type during a period when the Newf was a rare breed and almost unknown outside the dog fancy. The successful kennels of today have made use of the heritage from the "pioneers" who maintained and enhanced the breed during difficult times.

To the best of my knowledge, until 2002, Dryad Kennels was the oldest Newfoundland kennels still breeding in the United States. It began in 1940 by the Drurys in New York State. They had planned to name their kennel Drury Lane, but they loved trees and wanted a name related to the woods. Their choice was Dryad, named for a woods nymph. Following the death of Maynard, Kitty continued the kennels until 1970, when she turned the kennel name over to her daughter, the late Mary Dewey. Mary continued the Dryad name at her kennels in Colorado until her death in November 2002. Many, if not most, of the top winning and producing Newfs of today have Dryad's Sea Rover or Dryad's Goliath of Gath in the earlier generations of their pedigrees.

A contemporary *Dryad* dog, Ch. *Dryad's* Blackwatch Enforcer DD, DOB. Breeders and owners are Mary Dewey and Joan Gunn (pictured). Photo by Mike Reese.

Probably the most famous Newfoundland in American history is the dog, Seaman, sometimes known as Scannon, that accompanied Lewis and Clark on their 1803-1809 exploration of the American West. Seaman is mentioned a number of times in the journals of the expedition, which was commissioned by Thomas Jefferson, President of the United States at the time. On January 18, 2003, the official "kickoff" of the Lewis and Clark Bicentennial was held at Monticello, Jefferson's home. Seaman was honored by the presence of Newfoundlands that had been invited to attend and by an address by Dayton Duncan, master of ceremonies. Mr. Duncan is the author of two books on Lewis and Clark, as well as writer/co-producer of the PBS documentary on Lewis and Clark. Below is the text of his address:

You have probably noticed these large shaggy dogs circulating among you today. They are Newfoundlands, the same breed of dog that belonged to Captain Meriwether Lewis and accompanied him to the Pacific and back.

Captain Lewis bought his dog, named Seaman, for 20 dollars at the beginning of the journey—and described him in his journals as "very active, strong, and docile." The Indians, Lewis noted later, were impressed by what he called the "sagacity" of his big Newf.

Seaman's adventures are chronicled numerous times in the journals—encounters with an angry beaver, catching an antelope, barking at grizzly bears prowling nearby at night, and scaring off a buffalo bull that stampeded into camp one evening and nearly trampled some of the men. Of course, like everyone else, Seaman suffered on the journey—his paws were punctured by prickly pear cactus and his eyes and ears were the frequent targets of swarms of mosquitoes.

Big as he was, Seaman, however, was apparently never considered a candidate for dinner.

The last specific mention of Seaman in the journals is at the Great Falls in Montana on the return trip, being plagued again by mosquitoes. "My dog even howls with the torture he experiences," Lewis wrote.

Because Seaman isn't mentioned again, we can't say with absolute certainty what happened to this active, strong, and loyal member of the Corps of Discovery.

But, many people—myself included—believe he was standing on the deck of the white pirogue, barking with joy and his big tail wagging, when the expedition made its triumphant return to St. Louis in 1806.

Thank you Debra Thornton and the Colonial Newfoundland Society for joining us this morning.

Sir Edwin Landseer immortalized the Newfoundland in his paintings. His best-known Newf painting, "A Distinguished

Member of the Humane Society," painted in 1837, features the white and black Newfoundland which became known as the Landseer. (Today the Landseer is bred and shown as a separate breed in Europe. Europe still has white and black dogs, bred and shown as Newfoundlands. In the United States, white dogs marked with a specific pattern may be referred to as Landseers, but they are shown along with white and black dogs that do not fit the Landseer description.)

The well-known painting, "Madame Charpentier and Her Children," by Auguste Renoir, shows a child seated on a white and black Newfoundland dog. Many paintings by lesser artists and prints by Currier and Ives from the Victorian era can be found in antique shops and attics, attesting to the popularity of the Newfoundland during that period.

The AKC classifies the Newfoundland as a working breed. He was a true working dog on the island of his origin, long before he was formally defined as such. In his native home, the population used him to suit whatever needs they had for large, strong, tractable dogs. Traditional tasks included hauling cartloads of fish from the docks for fishermen, or hauling fish, milk or whatever products vendors might wish to sell from their carts. Wood was used for cooking and heating, and it had to be cut and hauled from the woods. Newfs were harnessed to sleds for this task. Like logging for lumber, this work was done mostly in winter because it was easier to haul the heavy weight over snow.

References to Newfs being used by fishermen to haul in nets do not describe how this was done, and it seemed like romantic fantasy to me. It was hard to imagine a dog would be of much use in pulling a heavy net full of fish into a boat—a task better suited to humans with hands and winches. However, while viewing a film of Atlantic fisherman using nets from the shoreline, I found a possible explanation of how the dogs may have been used in this task. One end of the

Lewis and Clark Bicentennial "Kick-Off" at Monticello. Several Newfs were lined up on the stage next to the podium as Dayton Duncan gave his talk on Seaman, the Newf who accompanied the "Corps of Discovery." Photo by Marvin Thornton.

Debbie Thornton's Newfs, Ch. *Cypress Bay's* Kiss and Tell and CH *Cypress Bay's* Southern Bell, are admired at the Bicentennial. Note that in keeping with the event, the gentleman petting the dogs is dressed in a Hudson's Bay coat and deerskin leggings. Photo by Marvin Thornton.

While hauling Christmas trees is not as difficult as hauling wood, CH *Hickory Ridge* Sir Lancelot and *Dorlin's* Northern Light carry on the tradition of hauling for owners Mike and Sandee Lovett. Photo by Sandee Lovett.

A Douglas fir tree "debarked" by one of the author's Newfs. A yardstick shows the height he managed to reach. Fortunately, the damage goes only about three-fourths of the way around the tree. Photo by author.

net was attached to a post driven into the beach. The fisherman would then row out, taking the other end of the net with him. Finally, he would circle back to shore. It is not a far stretch to imagine that a dog could be harnessed to the returning end of the net and help pull it in alongside the fisherman.

There was little sentimentality toward animals in earlier times, compared with the way Western cultures view them today. We like to think of working dogs as willing assistants acting out of devotion to their human "masters." Although there were owners who thought of their dogs with affection and treated them well, the reality of the times would suggest that the dogs were used, and sometimes abused, in a hardscrabble land where eking out a living meant heavy toil for human and beast alike.

The dogs were supposedly turned loose to fend for themselves during off-seasons when their work was not needed. How they subsisted is puzzling. Wild carnivores are taught by their mothers to catch and kill game, but carnivores reared in captivity and domesticated canines normally do not know how to hunt. Wild animals that have been rescued by humans cannot be released into the wild to make a living for themselves without some kind of "instruction." Wildlife experts often prepare young carnivores they have cared for to fend for themselves by using road kill as a starter. We can assume that no such preparation was given the Newfoundlands set loose to fend for themselves.

Dogs used by fishermen were maintained on fish and would have had the opportunity to learn to catch some for themselves. Dogs at Edenglen Kennels, belonging to the late Helena and Willis Linn in New York State, caught fish for sport in the natural pool fed by a stream at Edenglen. So, it is not difficult to think that the dogs in Newfoundland could have done the same thing. Perhaps humans sometimes threw a rabbit or squirrel carcass to the dogs, giving them some concept of these animals as food.

It is said that the Newfoundland dogs ate the cambium layer of trees—the most digestible part. Although the canine digestive system is designed to digest meat and entrails, hungry dogs would probably eat almost anything to fill their bellies. We know that dogs chew bark for amusement. We have had to put wire mesh around certain trees to stop some of our dogs from eating the bark and killing the trees. Newfs will also chew on, and swallow, pieces of sticks they find in the yard.

It has always interested me that our Newfs eagerly eat so many different plant foods. Early in the season they begin picking apples off the trees that are hardly an inch in diameter, and they continue eating them until the season is over. They love most of the fruits and vegetables we give them, and they pick wild blackberries. One youngster discovered the berries on our English Laurel bushes. A call to our local poison control center assured me they were not poisonous, but the pits, if bitten into, would release cyanide. We decided to put fencing around the bushes, just in case.

We were puzzled one summer to see several dogs lying around a plum tree for several days. The mystery was solved when we saw the largest dog stand on his hind legs and jump up to snag a plum. The branch sprang back, bringing a cascade of fruit to the dogs waiting under the tree. This suggests that it is conceivable that the Newfoundland dogs fending for themselves could survive, perhaps barely, with a most unusual and varied canine diet.

Newfs also have been used as workers in more recent times. The late Bill Cochrane of Dory-O Kennels in British Columbia spent his young manhood in Nova Scotia. As late as the 1930s, he carried the mail using a Newf to pull it on a sled in winter.

Today, people sometimes train Newfoundlands as lifeguards and lifesavers. In France, teams of two dogs assist human lifeguards at some of the beaches. In their book, *Dogs with Jobs*, Merrily Weisbord and Kim Kachanoff describe how Ferruccio Pilenga

The late Bill Cochrane kept up his working tradition with Newfs at his Dory-O Kennels in British Columbia by building a Newf cart for his daughter. Photo by Marge Cochrane.

of Italy has trained his dog to assist him as a lifesaver. He has gone beyond the usual beach lifeguard training; his Newf, Mas, goes with him to rescue swimmers or boaters in trouble in situations where a boat cannot get to a victim quickly enough. The dog has been trained to leap with Pilenga from a police helicopter. Pilenga supports the victim's head while Mas tows them to shore. Pilenga has established a training school where together he and his dog train a future generation of Newfs and their handlers in this important work.

Newf fanciers who live on wooded land sometimes hitch their dogs to sleds to haul wood in the winter. Newfies have been used to help raise funds for charitable organizations by giving cart rides to children—something they seem to really enjoy. The task is the same as that performed by dogs of the Victorian era, when giving cart rides to young masters was a popular job for the family Newf.

In literature, Nana, the Newfoundland nursemaid in James Barrie's *Peter Pan*, surely was inspired by the Newfs natural "tending" instinct:

It was a lesson in propriety to see her
escorting the children to school, walking

Am. Can. Ch. *Seabrook's* Sikome, owned by Garry and Pauline Baldwin, looks happier than her young passenger. Sikome has a draft dog title, among many other working titles. Photo by Garry Baldwin.

Examples of Newfoundland memorabilia: left, an antique bank; center, a replica of an antique nutcracker; right a contemporary doorstop made in St. Johns, Newfoundland. Photo by author.

sedately by their side....She proved to be quite a treasure of a nurse. How thorough she was at bath time....On John's soccer days she never once forgot his sweater, and she usually carried an umbrella in her mouth in case of rain.

Though whimsical, the description of Nana's behavior toward her charges carries a strong element of truth. Newfs are watchful of children, especially near water.

There are a number of children's books featuring Newfoundlands. Some of the more recent publications include:

Seaman, by Gail Karwoski
Newf, by Marie Killilea
The Lighthouse Dog, by Betty Waterton
The Captain's Dog, by Roland Smith
Seasons of the Sea, by Mary Lou McGuiere
Emma and the Night Dogs, by Susan Aller
The Dog Next Year, by Cornelia McGrath
Star in the Storm, by Joan Hiatt Harlow

Some older books can be found only through dealers of discontinued publications. These include:

Sailor's Choice, by Natalie Carson
The Sorely Trying Day, by Russell Hoban
Pierre Pidgeon, by Lee Kingman
The Dog Crusoe, by R. M. Ballantine
Along Came a Dog, by Mindert de Jong
(The dog in this story is not identified as a Newfoundland, but the illustrations and behavior of the dog strongly suggest a Newf.)

One can also find a wide range of Newfoundland memorabilia, ranging from penny banks and figurines to postage stamps and clothing. Collectors can locate antiques and replicas in the usual places: antique dealers, estate sales, garage sales, and in attics. A wide variety of Newf items also are available from artisans and dealers in dog arts and crafts. At the Newfoundland National Specialty show, club members rent tables and booths to display and sell their Newfoundland arts and crafts.

THE BREED STANDARD

Vision of Excellence

3

EACH AKC REGISTERED BREED HAS A BREED standard that gives a visual description of the dog, as well as the dog's purpose and typical behavioral traits. The standards are written and revised only by the "parent club" which, in the case of the Newfoundland, is the Newfoundland Club of America. The standard is used as a guide by both breeders and judges. It provides a written picture of the ideal Newfoundland and, while no dog is one hundred percent perfect, the standard should be studied and memorized by anyone planning to breed or show dogs. Pet owners can measure quality and determine whether an individual is indeed a purebred by comparing him or her to the standard. By evaluating structure and movement against the breed standard, people who want a working dog can insure that the dog of their choice will be able to perform tasks specific to the breed such as draft work or swimming.

The original Newfoundland Standard was written over one hundred years ago. Although modifications have been made to clarify and explain, the essentials remain unchanged. Nevertheless, a breed standard is somewhat subjective. Each judge interprets the standard according to his own understanding, preferences and dislikes, and each breeder emphasizes in her breeding program those traits she feels are most important, so, over time, some variations in type will appear. The purpose of the standard is to pre- serve the function of the Newfoundland as a multi-purpose dog capable of heavy work, active on land and in the water, and a devoted, noble companion to children and adults alike.

OFFICIAL AKC NEWFOUNDLAND STANDARD

General Appearance

The Newfoundland is a sweet-dispositioned dog that acts neither dull nor ill-tempered. He is a devoted companion. A multi-purpose dog, at home on land and in water, the Newfoundland is capable of draft work and possesses natural lifesaving abilities.

The Newfoundland is a large, heavily coated, well balanced dog that is deep-bodied, heavily boned, muscular, and strong. A good specimen of the breed has dignity and proud head carriage.

The following description is that of the ideal Newfoundland. Any deviation from this ideal is to be penalized to the extent of the deviation. Structural and movement faults common to all working dogs are as undesirable in the Newfoundland as in any other breed, even though they are not specifically mentioned herein.

Size, Proportion, Substance

Average height for adult dogs is 28 inches, for adult bitches, 26 inches. Approximate

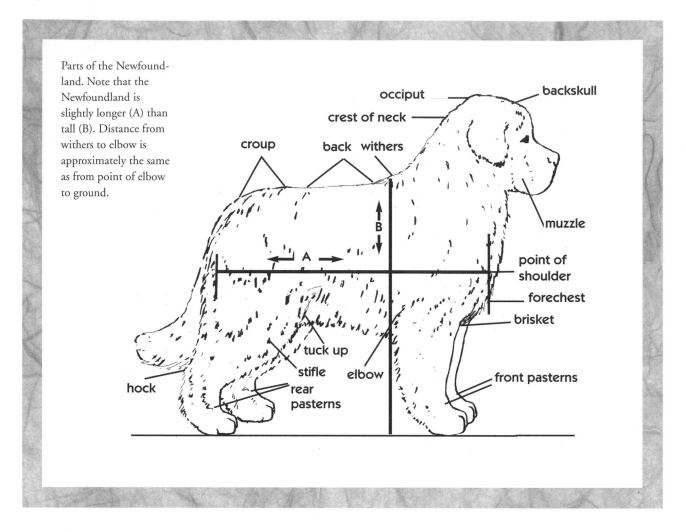

Parts of the Newfoundland. Note that the Newfoundland is slightly longer (A) than tall (B). Distance from withers to elbow is approximately the same as from point of elbow to ground.

occiput · backskull · crest of neck · croup · back · withers · muzzle · point of shoulder · forechest · brisket · tuck up · stifle · elbow · front pasterns · hock · rear pasterns · A · B

Ch. *Darbydale's* All Rise Pouch Cove, Best of Breed winner of three consecutive Newfoundland National Specialties, Best in Show at forty-three All-Breed shows, and Best in Show at the 2004 prestigious Westminister Kennel Club show. Photo by Ashbey Photography.

Ch. *Pooh Bear's* Bearabella, ROM. "Belle" was Best Opposite Sex at the '90 and '91 Newfoundland National Specialty shows. She is the dam of Ch. The Bombadier, ROM, top producing sire of 1995 and Ch. *Tabu Seabrook* Nobell Prize, DD, ROM, top producing dam of the same year. Owned by breeders Shelby Guclich and Lou Lomax, and Kathy Griffin. Photo by Anne Rogers.

Ch. John's Big Ben of *Pouch Cove,* ROM, (left) and Am. Can. Ch. *Pouch Cove's* Heritage (right) show the beautiful heads and expression called for in the standard. Both Newfs were bred by Peggy Helming. Ben, among the top producing sires, is owned by Peggy and Dave Helming. Hattie has several Water Test titles along with a Best in Show win. She is owned by Jan Boggio. Ben's photo by Soren Wesseltoft, Hattie's by Janet L. Wissmann.

weight of adult dogs ranges from 130 to 150 pounds, adult bitches from 100 to 120 pounds. The dog's appearance is more massive throughout than the bitch's. Large size is desirable, but never at the expense of balance, structure, and correct gait. The Newfoundland is slightly longer than tall when measured from the point of shoulder to point of buttocks and from withers to ground. He is a dog of considerable substance which is determined by spring of rib, strong muscle, and heavy bone.

Head

The head is massive, with a broad **skull**, slightly arched crown, and strongly developed occipital bone. Cheeks are well developed. **Eyes** are dark brown. (Browns and Grays may have lighter eyes and should be penalized only to the extent that color affects expression.) They are relatively small, deep-set, and spaced wide apart. Eyelids fit closely with no inversion. **Ears** are relatively small and triangular with rounded tips. They are set on the skull level with, or slightly above, the brow and lie close to the head. When the ear is brought forward, it reaches to the inner corner of the eye on the same side. **Expression** is soft and reflects the characteristics of the breed: benevolence, intelligence, and dignity.

Slope of the stop should be moderate but, because of the well-developed brow, it may appear abrupt in profile. Ears are relatively small and triangular with rounded tips, set on the skull level with, or slightly above, the brow and lying close to the head. Am. Can. Ch. *Nakiska's* Akavit, WRD, DD, bred and owned by Ingrid and Chris Lyden. Photo by Chris Lyden.

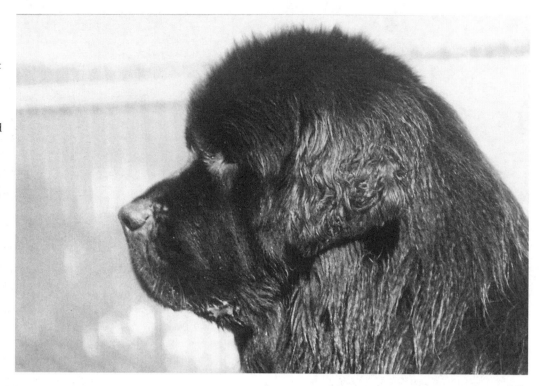

Forehead and face are smooth and free of wrinkles. Slope of the stop is moderate but, because of the well developed brow, it may appear abrupt in profile. The **muzzle** is clean-cut, broad throughout its length, and deep. Depth and length are approximately equal, the length from tip of nose to stop being less than that from stop to occiput. The top of the muzzle is rounded, and the bridge, in profile, is straight or only slightly arched. Teeth meet in a scissors or level bite. Dropped lower incisors, in an otherwise normal bite, are not indicative of a skeletal malocclusion and should be considered only a minor deviation.

Neck, Topline, Body

The neck is strong and well set on the shoulders and is long enough for proud head carriage. The **back** is strong, broad, and muscular and is level from just behind the withers to the croup. The chest is full and deep with the brisket reaching at least down to the elbows. Ribs are well sprung, with the anterior third of the rib cage tapered to allow elbow clearance. The

flank is deep. The croup is broad and slopes slightly. **Tail** set follows the natural line of the croup. The tail is broad at the base and strong. It has no kinks, and the distal bone reaches to the hock. When the dog is standing relaxed, its tail hangs straight or with a slight curve at the end. When the dog is in motion or excited, the tail is carried out, but it does not curl over the back.

Forequarters

Shoulders are muscular and well laid back. Elbows lie directly below the highest point of the withers. Forelegs are muscular, heavily boned, straight, and parallel to each other, and the elbows point directly to the rear. The distance from elbow to ground equals about half the dog's height. Pasterns are strong and slightly sloping. Feet are proportionate to the body in size, webbed, and cat foot in type. Dewclaws may be removed.

Hindquarters

The rear assembly is powerful, muscular, and heavily boned. Viewed from the rear, the legs are straight and parallel. Viewed from the side, the thighs are broad and fairly long. Stifles and hocks are well bent and the line from hock to ground is perpendicular. Hocks are well let down. Hind feet are similar to the front feet. Dewclaws should be removed.

Coat

The adult Newfoundland has a flat, water-resistant, double coat that tends to fall back into place when rubbed against the nap. The outer coat is coarse, moderately long, and full, either straight or with a wave. The undercoat is soft and dense, although it is often less dense during the summer months or in warmer climates. Hair on the face and muzzle is short and fine. The backs of the legs are feathered all the way down. The tail is covered with long dense hair. Excess hair may be trimmed for neatness. Whiskers need not be trimmed.

Color

Color is secondary to type, structure, and soundness.

Recognized Newfoundland colors are black, brown, gray, and white and black.

Solid Colors: Blacks, Browns, and Grays may appear as solid colors or solid colors with white at any, some, or all, of the following locations: chin, chest, toes, and tip of tail. Any amount of white found at these locations is typical and is not penalized. Also typical are a tinge of bronze on a black or gray coat and lighter furnishings on a brown or gray coat.

Landseer: White base coat with black markings. Typically, the head is solid black, or black with white on the muzzle, with or without a blaze. There is a separate black saddle and black on the rump extending onto a white tail.

Markings, on either Solid Colors or Landseers, might deviate considerably from those described and should be penalized only to the extent of the deviation. Clear white or white with minimal ticking is preferred.

A Newfoundland skeleton.

A *Mooncusser* puppy with white feet and white on the chest, typical markings on solid color dogs. Photo by Steve Walker.

THESE FINE DOGS ARE EXAMPLES OF THE BLACK, BLACK WITH WHITE, BROWN, AND GRAY COLORS FOUND IN NEWFS.

Ch. *Nakiska's* No Choice About It, a black dog bred and owned by Ingrid and Chris Lyden. He has several Water Test titles as well as being a Best in Show winner. Photo by Steve Ross.

Ch. *Copperidge Nashau-Auke* Kiowa, a white and black dog owned by Jane Thibault. Photo by David Thibault.

Ch. *Ironwood's* R. Naish Ebontide, a brown dog, bred and owned by Vicky and Larry Hansen. Browns have a range of color from light to dark brown. They often have lighter furnishings. Photo by Animal World.

Ch. *Mooncusser's* Color Me *Pouch Cove,* a gray bitch owned by Jan Boggio. Grays also may range from very light to very dark. Some appear to be almost black. Like the browns, they may have lighter furnishings. Photo by owner.

A Landseer dog jumping in Agility class. Note the white legs and underbody. Kirador's the Mighty Quinn owned by Dejah and Steve Petsch. Photo by Temple Imaging Services.

Tibetan Masiff, Multi-Champion Vayu Mei Dan Ni A Soechavati, bred by A. D. Reusen, and owned by Martha Feltenstein. This dog has tan markings, which are occasionally found in Newfs. Photo by Douglas K. Loving.

Beauty of markings should be considered only when comparing dogs of otherwise comparable quality and never at the expense of type, structure and soundness.

Disqualifications

Any colors or combinations of colors not specifically described are disqualified.

Gait

The Newfoundland in motion has good reach, strong drive, and gives the impression of effortless power. His gait is smooth and rhythmic, covering the maximum amount of ground with the minimum number of steps. Forelegs and hind legs travel straight forward. As the dog's speed increases, the legs tend toward single tracking.

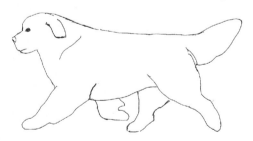

When moving, a slight roll of the skin is characteristic of the breed. Essential to good movement is the balance of correct front and rear assemblies.

This dog's muzzle is too long and lacks depth. Seen from the front, it also lacks breadth. The skull is flat and does not have a slightly arched crown. The stop is correct, but because the brow is not well developed, the stop appears too sloping. Ears are the correct size and shape, but are set too high on the skull. They should be set level with, or just slightly above the brow. Eyes are not deeply set, giving them a somewhat bulgy appearance.

This Newfoundland has a nice head, but the dog is faulty in several ways. Note that the body is excessively long and lacks depth, particularly in the loin. The rear legs are not fully feathered, making them appear light boned. The tail is not only curved, but is carried over the back. Perhaps this is a throwback to the Tibetan Mastiff, a possible ancestor of the Newfoundland.

Temperament

Sweetness of temperament is the hallmark of the Newfoundland; this is the most important single characteristic of the breed.

Disqualifications

Any colors or combinations of colors not specifically described are disqualified.

Approved May 8, 1990
Effective June 28, 1990
Copyright The American Kennel Club 1990

Multi-Champion, Multi-Best in Show *Midnight Lady's* Especially For You. This Hungarian dog was the top producing sire in the United States in 2001. Bred by Zsuzsa Somos and Attila Soos. Owned by breeders and P. Helming, M. Massa, and B. Siklosi. Photo by breeders.

THE STANDARD FOR THE NEWFOUNDLAND
CLUB OF GREAT BRITAIN

General Appearance
Well balanced, impresses with strength and great activity. Massive bone throughout, but not giving heavy inactive appearance. Noble, majestic and powerful.

Characteristics
Large draught and water dog, with natural life-saving instinct, and devoted companion.

Temperament
Exceptionally gentle, docile nature.

Head and Skull
Head broad and massive, occipital bone well developed, no decided stop, muzzle short, clean cut and rather square, covered with short fine hair.

Eyes
Small, dark brown, rather deeply set, not showing haw, set rather wide apart.

Ears
Small, set well back, square with skull, lying close to head, covered with short hair without fringe.

Mouth
Soft and well covered by lips. Scissor bite preferred, i.e. upper teeth closely overlapping lower teeth and set square to the jaws, but pincer tolerated.

Neck
Strong, well set on shoulders.

Forequarters
Legs perfectly straight, well-muscled, elbows fitting close to sides, well let down.

Body
Well ribbed, back broad with level topline, strong muscular loins. Chest deep, fairly broad.

Hindquarters
Very well built and strong. Slackness of loins and cow-hocks most undesirable. Dewclaws should be removed.

Feet
Large, webbed, and well shaped. Splayed or turned out feet most undesirable.

Tail

Moderate length, reaching a little below hock. Fair thickness well covered with hair, but not forming a flag. When standing hangs down-wards with slight curve at end. Tails with a kink or curled over back are most undesirable.

Gait / Movement

Free, slight rolling gait. When in motion slight toe-in at front acceptable.

Coat

Double, flat and dense, of coarse texture and oily nature, water-resistant. When brushed wrong way it falls back into place naturally. Fore legs well feathered. Body well covered but chest hair not forming a frill. Hind legs slightly feathered.

Colour

Only permitted colours are: -

Black: dull jet black may be tinged with bronze. Splash of white on the chest, toes and tip of tail acceptable.

Brown: can be chocolate or bronze. In all other respects follow black except for colour. Splash of white on the chest, toes and tip of tail acceptable.

Landseer: white and black markings only. For preference black head with narrow blaze, evenly marked saddle, black rump extending to tail. Beauty in markings to be taken greatly into consideration. Ticking undesirable.

Size

Average height at the shoulder: dogs 71 cms (28 ins); bitches 66 cms (26 ins). Average weight: dogs 64-69 kgs (140-150 lbs); bitches 50-54.5 kgs (110-120 lbs). While size and weight are important it is essential that symmetry is maintained.

Faults

Any departure from the foregoing points should be considered a fault and the seriousness with which the fault should be regarded should be in exact proportion to its degree.

Note: Male animals should have two apparently normal testicles fully descended into the scrotum.

Ch. *Numa's* Had To Be Pouch Cove, Best of Breed Winner at the 2000 National Specialty. Owned by Peggy Helming. Photo by Perry Phillips.

Ch. *Darbydale's* All Rise Pouch Cove shown winning Best of Breed at the 2004 Westminster Kennel Club Show. He went on to a coveted Best in Show win at this prestigious show. "Josh" is only the second Newfoundland, ever, to take the big win at Westminster. In addition to going Best of Breed at three consecutive Newfoundland National Specialty shows, he has forty-three Best in Show wins at All-Breed shows. He is owned by Peggy Helming and breeder, Carol Bergman. Photo by J. C. Photography.

CHOOSING YOUR NEWFOUNDLAND

Companion, Protection, Competition

4

THE PURCHASE OF A NEWFOUNDLAND represents a long-term investment of time and money and should be approached with deliberation. First, you need to consider whether you want a pet and companion, a protector, or a show dog. Do you want to participate in water or obedience competitions? Do you want a male or a female? Do you want a puppy or an older dog? What color do you prefer? You may not know the answers to these questions until you begin looking for a dog. Attending dog shows and observing Water Tests, visiting kennels, and talking to breeders and fanciers will help you make these decisions. If you are interested in getting an older dog or find the idea of giving a new home to a dog that someone else had to give up appealing, you can find dogs available through Newfoundland Rescue. A regional club in your area may have a rescue service with a dog or dogs available for adoption. The Newfoundland Club of America also has a rescue service. Information is on their website.

Most buyers want a Newf for one or more purposes which can be satisfied by any well-bred, healthy puppy that looks and acts like a Newfoundland. The buyer with showing or breeding in mind has a more difficult task in finding the right puppy. Showing and breeding require a considerable commitment of time and money, as well as a long learning process. If you are considering either, make a firm decision before you *begin* your search.

You may have a strong preference for one sex over the other. If this is not the case, either sex should be equally satisfying. Females (referred to as bitches) tend to be a bit more dependent, and males (referred to as dogs), more exploratory. Both are very oriented toward people and rarely show extreme favoritism for a single person in the family. Overall, dogs are larger than bitches and have proportionately larger heads. In the past, the drawbacks of a twice-annual heat season made bitches less desirable as pets than dogs. The availability of safe, inexpensive spaying has eliminated that problem.

Ch. *Nakiska's* No Questions Asked practices for a Water Test by retrieving a bumper. Bred and owned by Ingrid and Chris Lyden. Photo by Ingrid Lyden.

A five-month-old *Kilyka* puppy bitch, still wearing her fuzzy puppy coat. Bred by Karen Dunaway and Betty McDonnell. Photo by owner, Betty McDonnell.

Most people seem to prefer starting with a puppy. The joys of raising a puppy usually outweigh the disadvantages. However, under some circumstances a grown Newf should be considered. A working family, gone all day, will find that a typical mature adult dog will be more content when left alone than will an active puppy, and the adult dog will require less training to live in a household. Older or handicapped individuals will find a mature adult dog to be calmer and more easily managed. Families with very young children may find it easier to adopt an older dog that does not require the watchful tending required by puppies. Some young adult Newfs are quite exuberant, but by two years of age most are typical of the breed—calm, placid, and gentle.

Most Newfs adapt easily to a loving new family, and unless a dog has established some undesirable habits that are unmanageable, the adoption will be a success. The new owner should be advised of any health or behavior problems the dog might have in order to better cope with them. Some of the happiest adoptions have been with "problem" dogs nursed back to physical or emotional health by loving owners. However, it is an injustice to all concerned unless this kind of task is accepted with great deliberation. It may be possible to take an adult dog on a trial basis. Agreements regarding the return of a dog should be made *in writing* and *signed by both parties.*

Most Newfs are highly trainable and can succeed in various training activities such as obedience, tracking, water tests, carting, and backpacking. Some breeders are especially interested in these activities, encouraging their puppy buyers to participate and offering assistance and advice.

Any large dog with a deep bark offers protection for his family simply by his presence. This is the basic kind of protection most Newfoundland owners expect from their dogs. It is a mistake, however, to train a Newf as a guard dog, and it is surely an injustice to the dog. This breed is naturally trusting and gentle. It would require a traumatic change in the dog's basic character to turn him into a true guard dog.

When you are in the process of deciding what specific qualities you want in a Newfoundland, you will also be in the process of choosing a breeder from whom to purchase your dog. It is not always possible to visit a number of kennels. Newfs are rare in some areas of the country. In this case the best alternative would be to write to a number of breeders and telephone those whose responses interest you most.

Dog shows are an excellent place to learn about the breed and to talk with breeders and exhibitors. At any show there may be dogs representing a number of kennels from both local and other areas. Before the classes, exhibitors are preoccupied with

Six *Kilyka Newfs* with their flags. It would not be possible to take a picture such as this unless the dogs were highly trained, as these have been. Bred, owned, trained, and photographed by Betty McDonnell.

getting ready to show their dogs, so it is best to wait until after their Newfoundlands have been judged before talking with them. Breeders and fanciers with a wide range of experience will be able to answer questions about Newfs and offer information on available puppies and dogs.

Always call to make an appointment before visiting a kennel. Breeding dogs of good quality is a hobby rather than a business, and kennels usually are an adjunct of the breeder's home. There generally are no regular business hours at a breeding kennel and the prospective buyer is a guest, rather than a customer who comes at his own convenience.

Do not judge a kennel by the elegance of its facilities. Look instead to see whether there is adequate space for the dogs, appropriate shelter, security, fresh water, and general cleanliness. A few fresh stools are not an indication of carelessness, but old stools and odor may indicate a lack of care. Above all, watch the dogs. Even if they are not immaculately groomed, they should be glossy-coated, bright-eyed, curious, energetic, and responsive.

If there is a litter of puppies, their dam may be the least appealing of all the dogs.

Newfoundlands and friend behind the gate at Birgitta Gothen's *Ursula* Kennels in Denmark. Photo by Camilla Gothen.

Raising a litter is stressful and the dam may appear thin and out of coat. Do not judge the rest of the kennel on her less-than-usual-attractiveness.

Be cautious of purchasing a puppy from someone who has bred his or her pet dog to another pet. There is a greater risk of dissatisfaction in this situation than in getting a pet from a reputable breeder. Pet breeders rarely know the breed other than from experience with their own dogs. They do not know bloodlines, are unaware of genetic problems, may not know how to care properly for the dam and her puppies, cannot offer advice on raising puppies, and do not have a list of resources on health, training, and Newf activities. They may not know the protocol of selling puppies, such as sales agreements and guarantees, nor the AKC rules regarding registration. They do not keep up on canine literature concerning feeding, health, and immunization. They may have bred a litter thinking of earning a profit, and found the usual high costs overwhelming. Puppy diet, immunization, and health care may be sacrificed to make ends meet. Finally, the puppies may neither look nor act like typical Newfoundlands.

Beware of paying more for a puppy of a "rare" color. (See the chapter with the Official Newfoundland Standard.) Solid white, black and tan, buff, cream, and brindle colors will occasionally crop up, and such colors are not acceptable under the Standard. Serious breeders do not breed for unusual colors and they certainly do not charge more for them on the very rare occasions when they do appear. While these dogs may make suitable pets, they surely should cost no more than a puppy of a correct color. They may not be shown and should not be bred.

Buying a puppy from a pet shop holds the same hazards as buying from a pet breeder. In addition, the pup will have been exposed to other dogs and puppies at a time when his immune status is questionable. He will have been denied exercise and socialization while confined awaiting sale.

This is not to suggest that Newfs should be purchased only from large breeding kennels. Every breeder has to start small. A single-bitch owner who is learning about the breed, shows the bitch, and belongs to a regional and/or the national Newfoundland club, may produce excellent puppies. It is a breeder's commitment to the breed that determines the quality of the kennel. Many excellent Newfs are the products of beginning breeders.

No breeder can guarantee anything about a puppy except that his pedigree is accurate and his health is satisfactory at the time of sale. The puppy's genes and environment will determine his future health, temperament, intelligence, and appearance. If you are told that a puppy is a certain show winner, take heed. At best, a puppy can be described only as a show *prospect*. Even a gorgeous puppy with an impeccable pedigree can later develop faults that make him unsuitable as a show competitor.

Reputable breeders often have waiting lists for their puppies and buyers returning for additional purchases. They do not charge significantly higher or lower prices than other breeders. They do not try to make a specific dog or puppy seem more valuable because of a rare characteristic. (Usually, rare characteristics are undesirable because they do not conform to the breed Standard.) Many breeders will agree to replace or to refund money for a puppy that dies within a certain period of time or is unable to function as a pet because of genetic or congenital defects.

If one has confidence in the breeder, choosing the right pet from a litter is a matter of appeal. A breeder normally grades the puppies for show potential. Those considered show or breeding prospects may command a higher price or be sold only to buyers willing to show them. If there is a waiting list for the litter, those ordering show or breeding prospects will be offered first choice of puppies. Pet buyers may not be able to discern a difference between the pet and show prospects, particularly in a

VN and multi-champion *CastaNewf's* Mister November and *CastaNewf's* Cabot's Discovery, a dog with several Obedience, Water Test, Tracking, and Draft titles. Both dogs are owned by Christopher Firstner, pictured. The Newfoundland Standard calls for "dignity and proud head carriage," but Newfs are not above a little clowning when it pleases their people. Photo by Richard Newman.

uniform litter. Pet puppies will have been raised with the same care and concern for health and development as the show prospects.

If the litter is close enough to visit one or more times before a choice is made, the buyer has an opportunity to determine more about the puppies. A normally energetic pup may appear timid or restrained on the first visit, and a normally quiet pup may exhibit unusually high spirits. If you prefer either extreme, you should ask the breeder to confirm your assessment of a particular puppy.

Traits to avoid are timidity or shyness. A shy, fearful adult dog has an unreliable temperament and is to be avoided, even over an aggressive dog whose normal responses are a known factor. Fortunately, timidity, shyness, and aggressiveness occur infrequently in Newfoundlands.

When purchasing a show prospect, you should ask the breeder to help select a puppy. If you have made an effort to learn about the breed and approached the purchase of a puppy with care and deliberation, you will have chosen a particular breeder

with good reason. It is appropriate to trust that person's judgment as to the best puppy to select. If one or more pups are of comparable quality, the breeder will explain the strengths and weaknesses of each. At that point, you will need to decide which factors are most important, or simply which puppy is most appealing.

Breeding prospects must be chosen with equal care. Anyone interested in breeding obviously would start with a puppy bitch. Many breeders require that buyers of pet bitches sign an agreement to have them spayed. The same breeders selling breeding prospects may require certain commitments on the part of a first-time Newf buyer. Such commitments could include membership in a Newfoundland club, agreeing to show the bitch, allowing the breeder to choose a stud for a first mating, or requiring that the bitch be assessed for her merits as a brood bitch when she is full grown. The intent of such agreements is to protect the breed from indiscriminate breeding by individuals who are unconcerned for the future of the breed.

Males are not usually purchased for breeding purposes, although some people

buy dogs with that intent. Unless a dog is outstanding in quality, he will not be sought out as a stud dog. While it is appropriate to advertise in dog show catalogs and other dog periodicals that a stud dog is available, it is not considered proper protocol in the dog world to ask the owner of a bitch to breed the bitch to one's male.

Occasionally someone will plan to buy a puppy dog and a puppy bitch, intending to breed them at maturity. This is a mistake. The puppies might mature to be unsuitable mates. A breeder should attempt to compensate in one mate for the faults of the other. Owning a male and a female creates a great temptation to breed them despite the fact that such a mating may double up on certain faults. In addition, one or both dogs might not turn out to be of breeding quality. If you wish to begin with two puppies, it is far better to buy two bitches than to buy a male and a female.

If your bitch is of good quality, you will have a wide range of choices for a stud dog.

Finding the right stud will enable you to produce puppies as good as or better than your bitch. This is what breeding is all about. It is also far less expensive and less troublesome to pay an occasional stud fee than to buy and maintain a male. It is almost impossible to keep a male in the same kennel with a bitch in season unless you have special facilities. Even then, the male dog and the owners will experience considerable stress.

A well-bred puppy is the product of considerable investment on the part of the breeder. Each puppy represents expertise based upon years of study and experience, a sizeable financial outlay, and plain hard work. It is understandable that the breeder is as concerned with the placement of his or her puppies as the buyer is in choosing well. One of life's happiest moments is when a puppy or dog is turned over to his new owner after frank questioning and discussion has satisfied both buyer and breeder that each has made a good choice.

Following is a list of papers the breeder should provide the buyer at the time of sale:

1. A properly completed and signed individual AKC registration slip, or an agreement signed by buyer and seller as to when, and under what circumstances, the slip will be provided. The AKC requires that the registration slip is given with the puppy unless there is an agreement in writing to the contrary. Any contingencies upon which provision of the individual registration slip is based should be specifically and clearly stated.

2. A pedigree of three or more generations.

3. A sales agreement signed by buyer and seller describing the puppy, his sex, color and markings, litter number, date whelped, names and AKC registration numbers of sire and dam, agreements regarding guarantees, breeding or showing rights or obligations, spaying or neutering agreements, amount paid and installment payment agreements, and any other terms regarding the puppy.

4. Care and feeding instructions.

5. An immunization and worming history and schedule.

6. A current health certificate.

7. Copies of any veterinary health screening certifications on both parents.

A very young *Bjornebanden* puppy looks out at the world. Photo by breeder, Soren Wesseltoft.

YOUR NEW PUPPY

CARE AND TRAINING

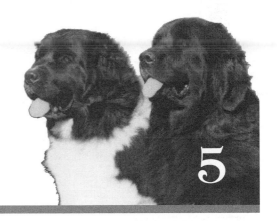

5

BRINGING HOME A NEW PUPPY IS THE climax of what may have been months of searching and planning. It is a moment of joy, excitement, and fulfillment. It is also a time of stress for puppy and owners. The normal order of a household becomes disrupted by the needs of a small, demanding creature that must adapt to a new and bewildering situation. Although many puppies are sent home with new owners at eight weeks, the most common age for Newf puppies to be turned over to new owners is between nine and twelve weeks. This is to allow for a final heart check. At this older age Newf pups are easy to housebreak if given frequent opportunities to go outside to eliminate.

HELPING YOUR PUPPY ADJUST

Much of that stress can be reduced if you prepare for your Newfoundland puppy *before* you bring him home. The most basic considerations are management strategies. Decide in advance which parts of the house the dog will be allowed in, where he will sleep, who will be responsible for housebreaking, feeding, and cleanup, where he will stay when no one is at home, and how he will be protected from hazards. Purchase supplies and equipment in advance. You will need food and water, puppy-safe toys and things to chew, and any equipment indicat-

ed by your management plan, such as a baby gate, crate, fencing, or a run.

One of the pleasures of owning a Newfoundland is the relative ease with which puppies can be raised to be good members of a household. They are easier to housebreak than many smaller, more active breeds, they have shorter spurts of activity, and they are relatively easy to train not to chew on forbidden things. If you have raised other breeds, you may be pleasantly surprised by your Newf puppy. Even so, constant vigilance is required for a few weeks.

Before you bring your new puppy home, decide how you will introduce him to his new home and family. He will most likely arrive in your car, either from the breeder's or from the airport if he has been shipped. Either way, realize that he will have suffered some trauma. He has just been removed from littermates or kennel mates, and from the people to whom he is closest. He has been removed from the surroundings, schedule, and habits he has known since he was old enough to be conscious of them. Suddenly everything is new and different. You should consider where your puppy was raised and where he will be kept in your home. If the weather is cold, and your pup was used to the cooler temperature of a kennel with an outside run, it may take some time for him to acclimate to a heated house. A Newfie puppy's fuzzy coat is very warm. If the puppy was raised in the house and you plan on keeping him in a garage or outside, consider keeping him in the house until he has adjusted to his new home, then gradually acclimate him to outside temperatures.

If the whole family has gone to pick up the puppy, he will have a chance to become familiar with them on the way home. After the car ride, the first thing your puppy will need to do is relieve himself. Do not put him down in an unfenced front yard and assume he will not dash into the street. He should be on a lead or carried to a safely fenced area. As soon as he relieves himself, praise him and take him into the house. This is the first step in housebreaking.

Once in the house, let the puppy explore in any areas that will not be off limits for him. Some pups are more curious than others and will explore eagerly. Others wait until they feel more at home. Some pups will stay by your side until curiosity overcomes timidity. After he has explored inside for a while, it is a good idea to take the pup outside again. This time, let him explore the yard for a bit, but be sure to praise him and take him inside immediately after he eliminates.

Keep water available at all times, but give the pup his first feeding according to his current feeding schedule provided by the breeder. You can change the schedule if necessary after the puppy feels more at home. Don't forget to take him out immediately after feeding. Our rule of thumb is that a new puppy is at home once he has eaten, drunk, urinated, defecated, and napped.

During the day, attention from his new owners distracts the new puppy from an awareness of the loss of familiar surroundings and the comfort of siblings. However, the first night, and sometimes for several nights, puppy and owner suffer from the trauma of changes in lifestyle. A ticking wind-up alarm clock and a soft pillow or stuffed toy may help substitute for the littermates the puppy is used to snuggling up to at night. Allowing the puppy to sleep in the same room as a human companion helps him feel less alone.

A crate provides a safe place for the puppy while you are asleep. Most puppies will accept being in a crate next to your bed

CRATES

Using a crate will help prevent accidents and aid in housebreaking. Puppies prefer not to foul their sleeping quarters and will learn bladder and bowel control. If you are determined to housebreak a pup as quickly as possible, set an alarm to go off several times the first few nights and take the pup outside to eliminate, thus encouraging his natural tendency to keep his sleeping quarters clean. Once acclimated to a crate, the puppy will consider it his own private retreat and security area. He can be kept there when you are away from home, when guests are present, or any time the family is too busy to keep an eye on him.

(left) A kennel or crate is ideal for both puppies and adult dogs. It is a safe place to keep a puppy when he can't be watched. A crate offers safety in a vehicle for dog and human, and is a "home away from home" for the dog while traveling. Photo by author.

(right) This wire crate is located in a busy area where a confined pup can feel less isolated while watching family activities. Photo by author.

To look at these innocent *Bjornebanden* puppies, you would think there wasn't an ounce of mischief in them. Photo by Soren Wesseltoft.

the first nights without crying or fussing as long as they sense your presence. A few calming words if the puppy whimpers will reassure him that you are nearby. This does not mean your puppy always has to sleep in the bedroom. Later, you can move his crate to the hall, and then to whatever sleeping area you choose.

If you prefer that the pup begin his new life in a designated sleeping area away from the owner's bedroom, the number of sleepless nights you will experience will vary from pup to pup. The puppy will adapt to this plan more readily if he spends some time there during the day learning to be alone, preferably in a crate. However, it may take longer for a puppy that is managed this way to bond to his human family. Give him safe toys for amusement and emotional security.

Except at night, with the crate next to your bed, training a dog or puppy to accept a crate takes time and patience. It may take several days of feeding, offering treats, and playing with the puppy while he is in the crate with the door open before he is ready to spend a very short time in it with the door closed. He needs to understand from the beginning that being put in the crate does not mean he will be there forever and that being put there is not punishment. He should associate the crate with pleasurable experiences.

PUPPY PROOFING YOUR HOME

Sleeping areas, as well as all other areas in which the pup will be allowed, must be made safe for him. Garages, laundry rooms, and kitchens all have their share of toxic materials that must be kept out of reach. Other hazards include small objects which might be swallowed, sharp or brittle objects that might be chewed, sharp projections, toxic plants, heavy objects that a pup might pull down upon himself, and open stairwells. A major hazard is electric cords, which are very appealing to puppies. There is usually no second chance to learn

Kilyka puppies get an early start in a pond at their breeder's kennels. These two seem to be taking their first dip quite seriously. Photo by Betty McDonnell.

the hazard of an electric cord once a pup bites into one. Sometimes a piece of furniture can be moved to block off a cord. You can purchase outlet covers at any hardware or department store. Be sure to check for cords under desks and computer stations. Make your computer room with its many cords and cables off limits to the puppy by using a baby gate. In fact, baby gates are an inexpensive way to keep a pup out of any area that may be hazardous to him or to your possessions.

Safe toys are a worthwhile investment. They provide amusement and satisfy a puppy's need to chew, and are also useful for socialization and training. In general, safe toys for puppies and adult dogs include hard rubber toys and balls, knotted socks, and nylon bones. You will find many other "puppy safe" toys at your local pet supply store. Children's toys are not safe for dogs as they can chew off and swallow parts of the toys. Unsafe toys include soft or hollow rubber balls and toys, golf balls, toys with bells, brittle plastic objects, and most raw or cooked meat bones with the exception of beef knuckles or marrow bones. Chicken and rib bones splinter and can kill a puppy.

TRAINING AND PLAYING WITH THE PUPPY

When a puppy picks up or chews on a forbidden object, tell him "No" in a loud voice and substitute a safe toy for the object. You can train the pup to give up objects by placing your hand over his muzzle and squeezing his mouth at the corners while saying, "Give." Squeezing will force the jaws apart so he will be forced to release his hold on the object. Praise the pup for giving.

Most Newfs quickly learn what they may and may not play with. We like to designate a puppy "toy box"—either a container or simply an area in a room where the puppy can expect to find his toys. This helps the puppy understand what is his to chew on and what is not. (Just don't expect him to pick up his toys at the end of the day!)

Most Newfs are natural retrievers, and puppies love to chase balls, sticks, and toys. This activity gives you a chance to play with your puppy and can be a training session at the same time. If a puppy does not return a retrieved object, squat down and encourage him to come. Most dogs that refuse to come when called will respond when the caller squats if they are rewarded with praise for coming. My neighbors think I can perform magic. When they are chasing their dogs that have fled the yard and won't respond to their commands, I go out, squat down and call to the dog in a high, friendly voice. Voila! I have a dog to hand over to them. Truly, this is a good thing to keep in mind. One day your dog may be in a situation when it is critical that he comes.

Never punish a dog when he comes to you. If he must be corrected for failure to come when called, go to him and correct him. If you have waited for him to come to you, praise him regardless of how long it took for him to come.

When the puppy returns a retrieved item, tell him to "Give," and take the item. If he refuses, squeeze the jaws just as you would with a forbidden object. It does not take much pressure to get the jaws to relax. Again, say "Give" and praise the pup. After many repetitions the puppy will learn to bring to you anything he may be carrying and to give it to you on command.

It is natural for puppies to pursue things that move. In the nest, they begin as early as three to four weeks to bite feebly at each other's tails and legs. As they grow, littermates play games of stalk and chase that end up with one pup tackling another, and both chewing and biting while struggling for a position on top. Presumably this is part of the inherent canine process of establishing the pack hierarchy, as well as practice for life as a predator in which skills of stalking, attacking, and killing are necessary for survival.

Young puppies will also mouth, chew, and bite at the moving parts of human feet, legs, and hands. Walking into a litter of five- or six-week-old puppies may require great dexterity on your part as you peel puppies off your pants legs in order to take the next step forward.

You may have heard the term "bite inhibition." This is an important trait for domestic pets. To some degree, puppies learn bite inhibition from their mother and siblings. The dam corrects pups that bite on her by growling or nipping them, and siblings will yip, squeal, and run away when a bite hurts.

You must teach a puppy that chewing on humans also is not acceptable behavior. Children and guests should be made aware that chewing, mouthing, and biting are not acceptable. If you do not want others correcting your puppy, remove him until he has learned not to do this. One way to correct biting is to give a sharp cry, move away, and ignore the pup, just as his littermates would do. This reinforces the idea that biting brings loss of attention and interaction. This process takes concentrated consistency. It can take a good many sessions before the pup learns not to bite. It is easy to overlook mouthing as harmless, but mouthing

and biting are parts of the same behavior pattern. Mouthing should be corrected in the same manner as biting until the pup learns that neither is acceptable. Sometimes a puppy will mouth or bite until corrected, then begin to lick you. This is a desirable response. Licking instead of biting should be rewarded with suitable sounds or words of praise.

Puppies, like children, will test to find out what limits have been set for them. Dams growl or snap at pups that have gone too far. Puppies use this same behavior to assert themselves. It is common for a pup to growl at a littermate when a bone or food is threatened. If a puppy growls at you when you reach for his food or toy, it is time to exert your leadership over the puppy. Never let him growl at you or anyone else whose actions the puppy should accept. (Some puppies develop a protective instinct at an early age, and growling might be appropriate under some circumstances, even for a puppy.) Immediate and firm correction is required, and should be repeated until the growling stops. A dog the size of a Newfoundland cannot be allowed to threaten you or anyone accepted by you.

While growling at humans is unusual behavior for a Newfoundland, even a puppy, do not be alarmed if your puppy growls when you try to take away his toy or food. He may not recognize you as his leader and is responding as he would to littermates trying to "steal" from him. If your puppy has never growled, it would be appropriate to set up a situation to give him the opportunity to do so while he is still small. Try to make the situation natural. For example, pick up his food dish while he is eating, or a toy or bone he is chewing on. Talk to the puppy, telling him you need to move his dish. Be cheerful, yet businesslike, and act as if you have a purpose in moving the dish, bone, or toy to another location. This will avoid any suggestion of teasing. Be sure to give the food, bone, or toy back to him in a new location a short distance from where you removed it. If the puppy growls, tell him "No" firmly and do not return what you have taken unless the growling stops. Repeat these provocations occasionally, and correct the pup if he growls until he learns that it is unacceptable.

Tug of war is a natural puppy game. However, the puppy should be the one to do the pulling so his stronger human playmate will not injure him. If he becomes aggressive and excited, stop. Desirable habits and attitudes should be encouraged in all play activities. Roughhousing with a puppy will not encourage him to be gentle. Children tend to play with puppies as they play with their friends, and must be taught to avoid rough play with puppies.

Decide on the limits you will set for your puppy and be consistent in enforcing them. Lack of consistency will confuse the puppy and make training difficult.

A very young *Midnite Bay* puppy. Note the enigmatic expression so common in Newf puppies. The soft, sweet adult expression develops with age. Photo courtesy of Jan Boggio.

LEASH TRAINING

A nylon or leather buckle collar is a necessity from the time a new puppy is brought home. It provides a means of restraining and guiding the puppy, and carries the license and identification tag. Check the collar on your growing puppy frequently to make certain it is not too tight. By the time he is an adult, a Newf puppy will have outgrown three or four collars. Training collars (slip collars) are for use only when a dog is on a lead. They should never be left on after the leash is removed.

When buying a lead for a puppy it is most economical to choose one that will last throughout his life. A four- to six-foot latigo lead is extremely durable. It should be three-quarters of an inch or one inch wide. Latigo is more supple than leather and is comfortable in the hands. It does not deteriorate from being soaked. Chain, nylon grosgrain, and cord leads are less expensive, but are hard on the hands when it is necessary to control a huge dog. If you plan to train your dog for obedience, choose a six-foot lead—the length required in most obedience classes.

Some puppies will accept a lead immediately and will trot along as if they had been perfectly trained. Others will become quite upset and fight the restraint. To prevent this possibility, put the collar on the pup, then attach the lead to it and let him drag the lead around the house. When the pup is accustomed to it, take him outside, pick up the end of the lead, and follow wherever he goes, putting little or no tension on the lead.

Gradually apply some light tension. When the pup is comfortable with this, encourage him to change direction by talking in a pleasant voice while giving a quick tug on the lead. Do not pull on the leash because this will encourage the puppy to resist. Give quick tugs and use your voice to persuade him to go your way, giving lots of praise when he does.

When the puppy is willingly walking with you, move briskly and change direction frequently. This will train him to watch where you are going in order to avoid the quick tugs he gets when taken by a surprise change of direction. The long-term benefit from a small effort in puppy training will be a grown dog that walks beside you without pulling and straining on the lead.

Not all puppies are alike, so it follows that not all puppies will respond in the desired way to the suggestions made above. However, these practices have worked well for us in training many puppies to live with us, and most have adapted well to them.

HOUSEBREAKING

Newfoundlands are not difficult to housebreak if you approach the process with consistency and concentration. Devote a week or two toward getting the puppy trained and avoid a long, drawn-out process that is hard on both you and the dog.

There are three basic principles in housebreaking: one, confine the puppy to a location where he can be monitored constantly; two, take him outside at appropriate times; and, three, confine him to a small area such as a crate or laundry room when you cannot watch him.

When the puppy is with you, watch for him to sniff the floor while moving at increased speed. Take him outside quickly, before he eliminates on the floor. If he does have an accident, say "No!" sharply, pick him up and take him outside. Wait until he eliminates again, praise him, and take him back inside.

Puppies should be taken out routinely after eating, after playing, and after a nap. A puppy under nine or ten weeks old can reasonably be taken out every half hour when he is awake. Taking him outside to the same place each time will help him learn what he is to do at that spot.

Never scold or punish a pup for an error you have not witnessed. He simply will not understand why he is being chastised. Consider the error your own for not watching him closely. Punishment and harsh scolding are not appropriate to the housebreaking process in any situation. Until a puppy is old enough to have control of his bladder and bowels, and until he has had sufficient training to understand what to do when he needs relief, he will do what nature demands. Between ten and twelve weeks, puppies are capable of better control and the frequency of urination is reduced. Many pups will stay dry and clean all night if confined to a small area, and most will have few accidents during the day if they have had consistent training for a week or two.

Physical punishment should be necessary only long enough to teach an understanding of the word "No." It is essential that a puppy learn this word early in his training, both for his own safety and for the well-being of the owner's property. Some pups have especially soft temperaments. A loud voice is enough to teach them the word "No." Others are more independent and may need a smack under the jaw for reinforcement. Obviously, the size and age of the puppy should be considered in determining the amount of force to use. Once the puppy responds to "No," physical punishment should not be necessary unless a command is disregarded or ignored. When housebreaking, use only the word "No." Do not use physical punishment.

An old spatula and dustpan work well for picking up stools from the floor that are not dry enough to be picked up with toilet tissue. Paper towels have the disadvantage of not being flushable. Urine on carpets should be blotted up first. Rubbing tends to spread and soak it further into the fibers. An excellent odor killer is a solution of twenty-five percent white vinegar to seventy-five percent water. After soaking up as much urine as possible, spray with the vinegar solution and rub it in well. This solution is safe for most fibers but should first be tested on a small area before being used on a regular basis. You can also find a number of products at pet supply stores that are effective for deodorizing and removing pet stains.

FEEDING

An experienced breeder will provide a diet and feeding schedule when your puppy is delivered. From eight weeks to six months puppies are usually fed three times a day. Your schedule may require a change in the times of day when the pup is fed. He will adjust to the change, but consistency is important. Mammals have a sense of time and a puppy needs the security of being fed when his "clock" tells him it is time.

It is best not to alter a pup's diet immediately. Before you take your puppy home, ask what brand of food he is eating and how it is fed—dry, mixed with water, etc. Stock up on the same brand before you bring home your puppy. If you have reason to change his diet, do so gradually by mixing in the new food in increasing proportions over several days.

Puppies are most expensive to feed during the year of rapid growth. A six-month-old pup will probably eat more than a two-year-old dog. Whatever the age, feed only premium foods found at pet supply stores rather than grocery store brands. Some smaller pet supply stores specialize in high quality and natural foods. There are foods especially formulated for large breed puppies. These are more suitable for Newfs than other puppy formulas. They have a lower fat content and some have lower protein. The idea is to keep growth at a slow pace in large and giant breeds.

Between eight weeks and six months of age, your Newfoundland pup will gain from three to five pounds per week. It is helpful to weigh the pup weekly in order to know when to increase his ration. If he gains less than three pounds per week, increase the amount at each feeding by one-half cup. Do not let a puppy gain four or five pounds per week on a regular basis. It is generally acknowledged that overfeeding is more dangerous than underfeeding. Overnutrition and overweight are separate conditions, though they may be found in combination. Overweight in adult dogs is harmful in the same way it is in humans. Overweight and overnutrition in a puppy can be devastating. Even if a pup does not develop a disease associated with overnutrition, additional weight on his fast-growing joints and ligaments can cause permanent damage. If in doubt about your puppy's weight and growth rate, consult your veterinarian. A rule of thumb for determining whether a puppy is too fat is to feel his ribs. They should not stand out, but should be easily felt without poking or prodding.

Self-feeding, or keeping dry food available at all times, was once an accepted practice based on the theory that dogs will regulate their own intakes. This feeding method is not favored today, especially for growing puppies. There are specific orthopedic diseases thought to be associated with overeating, and other diseases that may be exacerbated by it. Greedy or bored puppies are particularly at risk. They will eat all they can hold. Also, be aware that the recommended feeding amounts on dog food packages are often far more than your puppy will need to gain three pounds a week.

Some puppies seem hungry all of the time, creating the temptation to feed more than is necessary for proper health. There is also a temptation for first-time owners to get their "big" dogs as big as possible. Genes determine size, and unless a pup suffers from malnutrition, he will grow to his full potential on a moderate diet.

As with human diet, recommendations for canine diet have been undergoing changes. A change from mostly grain-based formulae to a meat-based one is one element that separates premium foods from other commercial foods. Breeders may suggest cottage cheese, yogurt or fresh meat as supplements to their recommended puppy diets. Although advocates of fresh food diets believe raw meat best meets the nutritional needs of dogs, there is also always the danger of E-coli, listeria, and salmonella. which unfortunately are all too common in meat and poultry.

Special utensils are not needed for food and water, but many owners prefer those made of stainless steel for durability and ease of cleaning.

Fresh water should be available indoors and out for dogs that spend time both places. A device that attaches to a hose or faucet permits a dog to drink at will without the need of a bucket or bowl. However, garden hoses are made with harmful materials that can leach into the water. If you use a drinking device or plan to fill an outdoor water bucket with a hose, use a hose intended for drinking water such as those available for travel trailers. Stainless steel is an ideal container for water, as well as for food. A galvanized bucket with a rough surface is difficult to clean and may leach zinc into the water. Enamel is easy to clean, but it chips readily. Plastic is satisfactory for adult dogs, but puppies often play with empty buckets and can quickly destroy plastic containers.

Newfs are untidy drinkers. Indoors, a water bowl or bucket may be placed in a newspaper-lined kitty litter tray or in a plastic dishpan. The paper will absorb splashes and spills and can be replaced as needed. This is also a good place to put the dog's food dish at mealtime.

Walking, jogging, and hiking all improve lung, heart, and vascular capacity in humans, but sometimes take their toll on the joints and feet. Your dog's joints and feet also are subject to injury. His footgear is what he is born with. Time is needed to toughen pads previously accustomed to lawn or carpet. Even pads that have been toughened are still susceptible to cuts, bruises, and damage from hot pavements.

Time spent jumping to catch balls and discs should also be increased gradually. Such activity involves the use of muscles, ligaments, and tendons not used in walking and running.

Newfs, with their fast-growing joints, need special consideration with regard to exercise. Soft cartilage is more susceptible to injury than adult bone. Prolonged or stressful exercise and play should be avoided during the rapid growth period of the puppy's first year. Giant breeds are more susceptible to joint injury than average-sized dogs during this period. Give your puppy a chance to grow up before including him in your hiking or jogging activities.

Children should not be allowed to play roughly or to pull, push, or press down on a puppy or grab him by the legs. Try to avoid letting your puppy leap from steps or

EXERCISE AND CONDITIONING

There are a few cautions to consider in providing exercise. Some joggers engaged in fitness programs like to include their dogs. Common sense dictates that a dog should not be expected to join a jogger who has worked himself up to a certain regimen unless the dog has had a similar period of conditioning. In warm weather, even a well-conditioned Newfoundland may not be able to exercise for his usual length of time because of his heavy coat and his inability to dissipate heat fast enough. A human dissipates heat over thousands of square inches of skin area. The dog's cooling system consists mainly of his mouth area through which he pants.

Early on a December morning in 1973, a well-known Newfoundland breeder in Nova Scotia was awakened by the bark of Whaler, an eight-month-old puppy. The house was on fire! The woman roused her two young daughters. One helped get all the dogs and a litter of puppies out of the house while the other ran for help. Whaler had been taken out with the other dogs but later ran back in, presumably to find the other child, who had gone for help. To their great sorrow, the family found that the puppy that had saved them with his alarm had perished in the house. They felt he had given his life in his attempt to save the girl.

furniture. Newf pups need not be kept in cotton wool, but in play, in exercise, and when being handled, reasonable consideration must be given in order to avoid unnecessary stress on the joints.

To lift and carry a heavy puppy, slip one hand under the rib cage so the hand supports the ribs with one or two fingers between the front legs. Lift the puppy so he is standing on his hind legs, then slip the other hand between the hind legs and lift. This method allows you to support the puppy without lifting him by the legs.

ROUTINE HEALTH CARE

Sometime during the first week you should take your puppy to the veterinarian of your choice for a physical and an examination for any possible hereditary or congenital problems. Even if the breeder had the puppy checked and provided a health guarantee, you should have the puppy checked for your own satisfaction, and to establish a schedule for booster shots, worm checks, and other routine care. You will probably want to have your puppy microchipped, as well. The chip is injected under the skin and each dog has his own number, which you can register in a national database. Lost dogs are routinely scanned for a microchip by most humane shelters. The owner's name and phone number are then found by contacting the registry.

Note the white on the chest of this charming *Pouch Cove* puppy. White on the chest is quite common and may cover an even larger area. Photo by Soren Wesseltoft.

Over the past few years, there has been considerable discussion as well as ongoing research within the veterinary community regarding immunizations. Only a few years ago there was a fairly standard protocol for immunizing both puppies and adult dogs. Now there is a range of opinion as to which vaccines are appropriate for the series of puppy shots, as well as the recommended frequency for boosters in adults. Your puppy's first shot was probably given at six weeks, and depending upon the age that you got him, he may have had a second. Be sure the breeder tells you which vaccines the pup has received and at what age. The breeder may have a recommendation that he or she has found successful for the booster shots. In any case, check with your vet for his or her recommendation as well. Distemper, parvovirus, and hepatitis are the core vaccines. Depending on the puppy's age and your location, your vet may recommend additional immunizations.

Puppies are usually vaccinated from three to four times by the age of sixteen weeks. Puppy shots are similar to annual boosters given to adult dogs, but are given at more frequent intervals because puppies receive temporary immunity from the dam's colostrum (the milk secreted after whelping) and the effectiveness of early immunization may be blocked by this immunity. The curve of maternal immunity drops off as the puppy ages. At sixteen weeks of age a high percentage of puppies will have lost this maternal immunity and will benefit from the effects of vaccines.

During the period between his first and final puppy shot, your puppy should not be exposed to dogs of unknown immune status. While it is not an ideal situation to keep a dog strictly confined to the owner's property, there is some risk involved in taking a young puppy to public places where other dogs have been. Canines gravitate to the scent of urine and feces, which are the most common transmitters of infectious canine diseases.

An eight-week-old puppy should have been checked for roundworms two or three

A white and black Bjornebanden pup and a black pup from the same litter. Note the slight white blaze on the head of the white and black pup. It is so slight, it may disappear with age, or it may remain. Either a solid black head or a blaze is acceptable. Photo by Soren Wesseltoft.

times. Follow the breeder's recommendations for follow-up stool checks, or consult with your vet. If your puppy is from an area of the country where heartworm is a threat, your veterinarian should advise you regarding preventive medication.

During the flea season, ask your vet for a safe puppy product. Flea bombs contain toxic ingredients. A borate-containing product is an alternative to flea bombs and is used on rugs and carpets, where fleas tend to lay their eggs. It is relatively safe if you follow the directions carefully.

GROOMING

Grooming your puppy with a weekly brushing will allow you to check for fleas and skin problems, as well as keep him clean and attractive. The puppy coat is a different texture from the adult coat. A pin brush or slicker brush works well for grooming the soft, fuzzy puppy coat. Nails should be trimmed as part of the grooming process, and ears cleaned if needed. (See the chapter on grooming for more detailed information.) Puppies should be bathed only when necessary.

Puppies begin to cut their permanent teeth, beginning with the lower incisors, between four and five months of age. Sometimes a permanent tooth will appear before the deciduous tooth has fallen out. If the baby tooth does not come out soon after the new tooth appears, check with your vet to see if the baby tooth should be removed. If it stays in too long, it can cause a misalignment of the permanent teeth.

A few Newfies retain the long, fuzzy puppy coat until they are eight or nine months old. Most have some adult coat beginning to appear by the time they are six months old. First, you will notice coarse, shiny hair coming in on the tail, about a fourth of the way from its base. Next, you will see shiny adult hair growing

At ten months, this *Midnight Lady* youngster has the look of both a puppy and an adult dog. Photo by breeders.

PUPPY

Doing his play bow,

The pup begins my training.

Soon we will be mates

Where he will choose the action,

And I carry out my roles.

Alan Riley

along the spine and the lower legs. Then the adult coat begins to fill in over the body.

From about seven to twelve months, Newfs go through what is referred to as the "uglies." They have lost the cute baby coat and appear leggy and awkward. Their body does not have adult depth and breadth, so the pups look rangy. Since their body parts do not always develop in synchrony, some puppies will be high in the rear. At about eighteen to twenty months, most Newf lose that unattractive, adolescent appearance. However, it takes up to four years for a Newfoundland's head and body to be completely developed.

SUMMARY

There may be times when you feel your life is on hold while you and the puppy learn to live with one another. You will find yourself constantly wondering if you remembered to put back the baby gate after you moved it, or whether the children left any toys on the floor that the puppy could harm himself with or destroy. You will be watching the puppy constantly for signs that he needs to go outside. After a few weeks of tension, things will improve. Just as it takes some time to establish a routine for a new baby, it will take a while to do the same with a puppy. Once you have a routine established, life will be much easier for everyone.

CARING FOR THE ADULT NEWFOUNDLAND

DIET, HEALTH AND HOUSING

6

As your Newfoundland matures, some of his care and maintenance needs will remain the same, while others will need to be adjusted. The first of those is his diet.

DIET

Adult Newfoundlands should be fed twice a day. If this is impractical, once-a-day feeding is acceptable. The dog should be given the opportunity to eliminate after feeding, but exercise should be delayed for an hour or more after eating. This helps to prevent bloat and other digestive disorders.

The most practical diet for a large breed adult dog is a premium quality dry commercial product. Most dogs will find commercial dry rations palatable, but beware of bargain brands. They are no bargain if they fail to meet the dog's nutritional needs. Instead, choose from the wide range of premium foods available. Most pet supply stores stock the premium foods. Others can be found only in specialty pet stores, and brands will vary depending upon your area of the country because distribution systems for specialized foods are often regional instead of national. Most brands offer a variety of diets specific to the age and condition of the dog. They may also have foods formulated specifically for large breeds. This is the best choice for Newfoundlands because it is balanced to meet all the nutritional needs of large dogs.

Many breeders and owners supplement up to one-fourth of the dry ration with canned or fresh meat. Others add vegetables to the diet. Unless they are cooked or finely pureed, raw vegetables go right through the dog's system undigested. Uncooked beef thighbones are probably safe, but cannot be left lying around for prolonged chewing. Bacteria contaminate them as the marrow and any attached flesh begins to decay. With E-coli found commonly in meat packing plants today, it is essential when feeding raw meat as a supplement or as part of a "home cooked" diet to determine that the meat comes from a reliable source and is fresh.

Some Diet No-Nos

Dogs should never be fed onions, which are toxic to canines. Garlic should be fed in small amounts only. Chocolate, especially the dark cooking chocolate, is also potentially toxic. Never feed rib or chicken bones to your Newfoundland as they can splinter and choke.

A balanced dry ration may not be adequate for all Newfs in all situations. Stresses such as extremely cold weather, prolonged periods of physical activity, illness, parasitic

Ch. *Pooh Bear's* Bearabella, ROM, shown winning the Veteran class at a Newfoundland National Specialty show at age ten. Belle won Best of Breed at a Newfoundland Regional Specialty show in 1995 from the Veteran Bitch class. Owned by breeders Shelby Guelich and Lou Lomax, and Kathy Griffin. Photo by Anne Rogers.

infestation, pregnancy, growth, and old age may make the usual ration inadequate in quantity or quality. Dogs kept outside in cold weather usually need additional calories to compensate for those burned in keeping warm.

Some signs of inadequate nutrition include harsh or dry coat, skin problems, reduced energy level, lack of appetite, increased appetite, excessive water intake, and coprophagia (stool eating). Since these signs may also be symptomatic of other problems, it is advisable to seek veterinary assistance. Even if nutrition is the problem, you must determine the specific deficiency before you can correct it. Random supplementation may only compound the problem.

Some diets tend to produce soft stools. Chronic soft stools indicate that food is passing through the digestive system too quickly and the dog may not be getting full nutrition from it. If a dog appears and acts healthy in all other respects, experiment with different brands of dog food until one

is found that produces normal, firm stools. Abrupt changes of food may cause diarrhea so it is always best to change foods gradually by adding the new food in increasing amounts over a period of several days. Chronic diarrhea is another matter. If diarrhea lasts more than a day, it is important to seek veterinary assistance.

There is a growing movement toward "home cooking" for dogs, but this should be approached only after careful research. It is not easy to create a balanced diet without expert advice. There are books available by individuals who have developed, and had success with, their own diets. It is necessary, though, to check on and to trust the credentials of the writers.

You can buy or construct raised "tables" for feeding large breed dogs. The idea is that there is less stress on the dog's joints, and gravity helps the food go down the right way. I know of no studies to support this idea, but it probably does no harm and may be beneficial. I might note, however, that wild canids, and most four-footed animals, eat while bending over their food.

Except when training, there is little or no justification for giving dogs treats on a regular basis. This establishes hard-to-break habits, encourages begging, and adds unneeded calories. First-time Newf owners tend to overfeed their dogs. For good health and longevity, Newfs must not be permitted to become overweight. Excess weight overtaxes the cardiovascular system and stresses the joints.

BLOAT

Large, deep-chested breeds such as Newfoundlands are susceptible to bloat, a potentially fatal phenomenon. The cause is unknown, despite significant research. The medical term for bloat is acute gastric dilatation. It is a syndrome typified by a swelling of the abdomen. In some cases, the stomach rotates (volvulus), cutting off its blood supply. However, distention of the abdomen due to the buildup of gases, even without stomach rotation, causes pressure on the vital organs and eventually leads to shock, then death. Early symptoms may include salivating, heavy panting, pacing, and a distressed look. Once a dog has begun to bloat, there is no chance of mistaking the problem. Emergency care is needed immediately. Without knowing the cause or causes of bloat, it is felt that the precautions of feeding two smaller meals, rather than one large meal, and restricting exercise after feeding, are well advised. Bloat is a potentially fatal condition and dog owners should consult their veterinarians about further preventive measures.

EATING PROBLEMS

Newfoundlands have a tendency toward pica (eating non-food items). Many are especially fond of wood, charcoal, or grass. The material swallowed seems to be tolerated by the digestive system. However, charcoal briquettes may have additives that could prove dangerous, and hardwoods tend to splinter. Grass treated with chemical fertilizers or herbicides can be toxic. It is wise to be aware of these possible hazards if one owns a wood-charcoal- or grass-eating Newf.

Stool eating, which may be caused by boredom, a nutritional deficiency, or a lack of sufficient digestive enzymes, can become a habit that continues even after the causative factors have been corrected. Dogs can pick up the habit from one another. While the vice has been described as "a rather harmless way a dog recycles food," it is repugnant to humans and could be harmful to a dog that consumes waste from dogs with parasites or other diseases spread through contact with feces. Once a dog develops this habit it is important to keep stools picked up and to follow the regimen prescribed by a veterinarian.

VN Ch. *Dryad's* Onyx Tinkerbird At *Blackwatch*, bred by Dryad Kennel and Darien Morrison. Owned by Dryad Kennel and Joan Gunn. Photo by Sandy Donnay.

SHELTER AND PROTECTION

Newfoundlands that are housedogs need no special shelter. Dogs kept outdoors, either regularly or occasionally, do need shelter from rain and direct sun. Cold is rarely a problem with this breed. Many Newfs choose to lie on a snowy deck or patio rather than in a doghouse, even in zero-degree weather. A doghouse should be out of the wind and raised off the ground.

Newfoundlands, like all pets, are dependent on the protection that only the owner can provide. Breeders usually require that prospective puppy buyers have a fenced yard or run. Unfortunately, if a single dog is expected to spend most of his time alone in a run, the possibilities for exercise are limited and boredom is inevitable. A run can be an ideal place to keep a dog when the owners are gone, especially if he can exercise in a fenced yard or spend time in the house when his owners are home.

Some Newfs are diggers and this trait should be considered when fencing a run or yard, especially if a dog is left alone in these areas. Extending the fencing in an underground trench makes digging out more difficult. A concrete base for a run eliminates the digging problem but stays wet from rain and urine. Four to six inches of pea gravel is preferable from the standpoint of both drainage and sanitation. Both concrete and gravel can be sanitized and deodorized with a mild solution of water and chlorine bleach.

Dogs should never be chained. Chains or ropes can be hazards in themselves. In addition, the dog is at the mercy of any person or other animal that might harass or harm him. The danger is not only physical, but emotional as well.

Under no circumstances should a dog be allowed to run loose. It isn't fair to the dog, the neighbors, or passers-by. The dangers to the dog are obvious: motor vehicles, poisoned or contaminated food or water, irate humans, and the possibility of theft or becoming lost.

TRAVELING WITH YOUR NEWF

Many devoted dog owners regularly take their dogs with them in the car. Most Newfs welcome the opportunity for a change of scenery. The best way to carry a dog in any vehicle is in a portable crate or kennel, which offers protection for both dog and human in case of a sudden stop or an accident. Compact vehicles will not accommodate a crate large enough for a Newf. Removable grilles, available through pet supply shops, act as a barrier between the rear of a station wagon or SUV and the passenger seats. Seat belts for dogs may be your only choice in a sedan. Since these are not government tested and approved like child safety seats, it is up to the buyer to determine which one might be safest for his or her dog.

Any animal as large as a Newf can make changing lanes or backing up hazardous because he obstructs the driver's rear vision. Train your Newf to lie down on command while in a vehicle. Never allow him to ride with his head out the window. This not only

Newfoundlands are nurturers, both with young things and with adults. When Teddy was seven months old, a new litter of puppies appeared on the scene. When the babies were old enough to go into an outdoor run during the day, Teddy would jump over the barrier into the run. Although still a puppy himself, he would lie down with the babies, which were about five weeks old, and let them bite and tug on him. He gently played back. The puppies often went to sleep on him. When he was ready to leave, he carefully got up without disturbing his charges and jumped back over the barrier.

Teddy had an unusual way of communicating. If the car keys came out and he hoped to go along, if it was his dinnertime and his owners were not tending to business, or if he was uneasy with a situation, his owners would feel a warm paw hooked around one leg in an anxious, but firm, embrace.

He loved company and when he became senior dog in the household he was often allowed to be with the guests. Even non-dog lovers became enchanted when he would sit down beside them on the sofa with his bottom on the cushion and his forefeet properly on the floor. One evening Teddy was sitting next to a guest who was describing an unhappy family situation. He seemed to sense her distress, and breaking his own rule of "feet on the floor," he lay over and put his head in her lap. His comforting gesture was received gratefully.

interferes with the driver's vision, but can cause injury to the dog's eyes and ears.

Cars parked in the sun become extremely hot, even on cool days. A slightly open window or windows will not be adequate to cool and ventilate the car on sunny days. On warm days, a car can become dangerously hot even with all the windows open unless it is parked in the shade. It takes only a brief time for a car parked in the sun to become a death trap for a dog. Never leave your Newf in a parked car during warm or hot weather.

Frequently, dogs are seen riding in the backs of open pickups. There is no way to tether a dog safely in a pickup without running the risk of injury in the event of a sudden stop or a rear end collision. Untethered, the dog faces the same risks and is free to jump out of the vehicle. Regardless of how well trained a dog might be, a bitch in season or some other attraction can prove to be a fatal lure. If you must carry your dog in a pickup, he should be crated and provided with protection against sun and rain.

HEALTH CARE

Today you will find many available choices in veterinary care. Doctors of veterinary medicine (DVMs) practice traditional veterinary medicine. Among their ranks are specialists such as surgeons, orthopedists, eye specialists, and internal medicine practitioners, oncologists, and more, much as in human medicine. Practitioners of alternative medicine specialize in acupuncture, homeopathy, holistic medicine, chiropractic, or sometimes a combination of these. Some DVMs have also studied alternative medicine and can offer treatment in both traditional and alternative protocols.

Routine veterinary care includes immunizations and annual checkups. The series of puppy vaccinations mentioned in the previous chapter does not provide permanent immunity. Until fairly recently, annual booster shots have been routinely recommended.

A PORTRAIT GALLERY

An adult bitch, VN Ch. *CastaNewf's* Front Page News, bred and owned by Denise and Marc Castonguay. Photo by Amanda Galloway.

An adult male, VN Ch. *Kilyka's* Daddy Dakota Sport, owned by Lori and Stan Peznowski. Photo by owner.

Currently we are in the midst of some controversy regarding this practice. There is now a concept of "over-vaccination," which some veterinarians believe can lead to autoimmune disorders. Research is ongoing to try to determine a recommended protocol, but it may be some time before any conclusion can be reached. In the meantime, it is best to follow the recommendations of your chosen veterinarian.

Most localities have laws requiring proof of rabies vaccination. After a puppy's

Kilyka's Jamielee, owned by Zoe Montague, is in the river, on her way to get to a swimming hole. Photo by Robert Carpenter.

initial rabies vaccination and a follow-up booster a year later, the dog will not need another rabies shot for three years if vaccinated with a product certified for that length of time.

The normal body temperature of dogs is 101.5 degrees Fahrenheit. It is easiest to take a dog's temperature using a rectal thermometer if someone is available to assist in distracting the dog by petting and talking to him during the process. Begin by lubricating the thermometer with petroleum jelly or tepid water. Then "down" the dog and turn him on his side. While he is being distracted, lift the tail and insert the thermometer. Hold it in place for three to five minutes, then remove it and praise the dog. Digital thermometers are now very reasonably priced and, unlike glass thermometers, are unbreakable. They are easier to use, and some "beep" when they have reached the correct temperature, signaling when to withdraw them.

A change in behavior often warrants veterinary attention. Sometimes it takes a day or two for the owner to become aware that a dog is not feeling well. Refusal of a single meal is not going to send one running

to the vet, but a second day's refusal or noticeable behavior changes would indicate something is amiss. Projectile or bloody diarrhea, projectile or persistent vomiting, inability to keep down water, rigidity or paralysis, convulsions, breathing difficulties, unusually heavy panting, bloating, excessive or frothy salivating, and obvious pain are all indications that your Newf needs immediate medical attention.

Large breed dogs are stoic in the face of pain. If your dog is whimpering, crying out, or limping severely, he is probably in considerable pain. The reason for such behavior may not be apparent. It is far better to have the dog examined than to delay seeking advice on what could be a life-threatening problem.

Skin problems make up the largest percentage of client visits to many veterinarians. They may be caused by fleas and other parasites, both internal and external, and by allergies, fungi, trauma, and irritations. Diagnosis of the causative factor is necessary before appropriate treatment is begun. Because these are not life-threatening, it is tempting to wait for skin problems to clear up by themselves or to try home remedies.

Three Newfs, owned by Mary Jane Spackman, at home in the water. *Pouch Cove's* A Rose is a Rose, TD, on the left, is the mother of Ch. *Pouch Cove's* Say Your Prayers, center, and Ch. *Pouch Cove's* By Any Other Name on the right, both of whom hold Versatility titles. Photo by owner.

However, if neglected, most skin problems only become worse. It is more economical for the owner and more comfortable for the dog to have skin problems treated before they get out of hand.

ORTHOPEDIC PROBLEMS

Large and giant breeds are more susceptible to orthopedic problems than smaller breeds. Some of these problems are transmitted genetically, and some seem to be the result of a familial tendency. Some occur because of trauma. The usual symptom of an orthopedic problem is lameness. A puppy or dog may limp as the result of a cut pad, a foot fungus, or a minor trauma. If a limp persists longer than a day or two, consult a veterinarian. Surgery, rest, or medication may be indicated, depending on the diagnosis, and the sooner the better.

Limping in the forequarters could indicate osteochondritis dissecans, a condition in which a lesion occurs in the growth area of one of the long bones. It is a juvenile disease. It is thought to be a result of trauma (such as

jumping from a raised object) that occurs in puppies with a familial tendency toward the disease. If the lesion is severe or if a fragment of bone has chipped off, surgery may be necessary. Less severe cases may be overcome with a restriction of activity.

Another forequarter problem is elbow dysplasia. This condition involves more than one phenomenon. Usually, elbow dysplasia involves failure of certain elbow bones to unite during growth. Surgery is required to remove loose bone.

Long bone disease, or panosteitis, can affect all four limbs. In many cases, a limp will "travel" from one leg to another, or to all of the legs. Like osteochondritis and elbow dysplasia, panosteitis begins in puppyhood. It is considered self-limiting, and most dogs recover by a year to eighteen months of age. Analgesics may be prescribed to alleviate discomfort. Do not administer analgesics without advice from your vet. Dogs can tolerate aspirin, but it is hard on the stomach. Enteric-coated aspirin is rather ineffective in dogs because of their shorter digestive tracts. Buffered aspirin might be used temporarily at night or over the weekend when your vet cannot be reached. Under no circumstance use any brand of acetaminophen: It is toxic to dogs.

Hindquarter lameness is most often associated with hip dysplasia. This is a hereditary disease that ranges in severity from mild to extreme. A dog with mild or moderate dysplasia may go through life never showing symptoms. Other dogs show symptoms as early as four or five months of age. Common early symptoms include difficulty in getting up from a prone position and "bunny hopping" rather than gaiting. Older dogs with no previous symptoms may show stiffness or have difficulty in getting up after exercise. Hip dysplasia is a progressive disease in which the femoral head becomes misshapen and does not fit tightly into the hip socket. Surgery can sometimes alleviate the discomfort of the disease.

A ruptured cruciate ligament in the stifle (knee) also causes hindquarter lameness.

This condition is thought to be caused by trauma. If the rupture is complete, the dog will usually put no weight on the leg. With partial ruptures some dogs will show only occasional lameness. Surgery is usually required to repair the injury.

Forty to fifty years ago many orthopedic diseases were virtually unknown to the veterinary general practitioner. The increase in popularity of the large and giant breeds since then has brought an increase in knowledge of these diseases and how to diagnose and treat them. Obviously, a veterinarian with a large clientele of giant breeds will have had more experience in radiographing, diagnosing, and treating these diseases. It is worth making an effort to find such a veterinarian, not only for his or her experience with orthopedics but because of familiarity with general care and treatment of the giant breeds.

EXTERNAL PARASITES

Dogs are hosts to a variety of external and internal parasites. The most common external parasites are fleas, which are seasonal from summer to early winter. Fleas cause great discomfort and act as hosts for diseases and worms. Dogs with a heavy infestation or with a flea allergy become frantic with the itching and can scratch and chew on themselves to the point where the skin becomes severely damaged. It is not always possible to find fleas on a heavy-coated dog, but if he is scratching and chewing they are probably present.

The best way to avoid the problems caused by fleas is to keep them under control. This includes trying to eliminate fleas and eggs from the dog's environment as well as from the dog himself. Chemicals in the environment can be harmful, so it is wise to use only those products recommended by your veterinarian.

If your dog is scratching and you find a number of pustules or a lesion, have the dog examined by your vet. Without relief from the itching, the dog will irritate these areas

Ch. *Midnite Bay's* Smart Asset managed to stay out of the river long enough to pose for his picture. Owned by breeder. Photo by Jan Boggio.

to the point where a "hot spot" develops. The skin exudes a thick, oily substance and becomes very sore and tender. Continued irritation will cause the hot spot to enlarge and become infected. The hair around the hot spot is usually clipped to expose it to the air and an antibiotic ointment or a topical anesthetic may be prescribed.

Ticks are another a serious problem in some areas during the summer. Ticks carry several diseases. They tend to lodge behind the ears or in the armpits, but can attach themselves to any area of the dog's body. Examine your dog's skin frequently to find the ticks before they become engorged. One disease spread by ticks is Lyme disease, which affects dogs and other species. It is carried by the deer tick and is becoming a problem throughout the United States. Your veterinarian may recommend an annual vaccine. If you plan to travel or hike with your dog in wooded areas where the disease is present, you should ask to have him vaccinated.

Mange mites usually infest the skin around the eyes and mouth. The mites cannot be seen and their presence is indicated by loss of hair. Your vet can prescribe a suitable medication for treatment.

Ear mites are indicated by a foul odor and a rapid buildup of a dark exudate in the ears. The dog may shake his head and scratch his ears. Discovered early, ear mites usually are not difficult to eliminate. An untreated, long-standing case is more difficult to treat successfully.

INTERNAL PARASITES

Roundworm is the most common internal parasite found in dogs. Mature roundworms can be found in most puppies before six weeks of age. Left unchecked, they can severely debilitate a growing pup. Repeated wormings are usually necessary before all adult worms and eggs are expelled.

Hookworm, whipworm, and tapeworm are also intestinal parasites. Although less common than roundworms, they are se-

Bearcove Coastguard, owned by N. Clarke, carries his little Poodle friend in his pack. Photo by Anne Rogers.

verely debilitating to both puppies and adult dogs. Dogs become infested with tapeworm by eating fleas that harbor tapeworm eggs. A less common source is uncooked meat. Whipworm and hookworm are contracted from feces of infected dogs or from soil on which such feces have decayed. Whipworm eggs attached to pads or coat are licked off and ingested by the dog. Hookworm larvae penetrate the dog's pads and enter the bloodstream and ultimately the intestinal tract. Yards and kennels must be treated in addition to treating the dog.

Worming medications for these parasites are available only through licensed veterinarians. It is advisable to have your dog's stools checked by your vet every six months and to follow his or her advice for treatment. Worming a dog with patent medicines for undiagnosed parasites is taking an unnecessary risk with your dog's health.

Once a dog has contracted hookworm or whipworm, sanitation practices become doubly important. The dog can become reinfected from his own droppings. Your vet can advise you of a regimen to follow to prevent reinfection.

SOME USEFUL TIPS GLEANED FROM EXPERIENCE

- Save worn and torn terry towels and washcloths of all sizes. They are invaluable if you own Newfies.

- Keep a hand towel or washcloth in the glove compartment of your car for wiping your dog's mouth as needed.

- Keep a hand towel or washcloth in your pocket when you walk the dog or take him to the vet. Anyone who wants to pet the dog will be grateful not to have to wipe slobber from clothes and hands.

- Keep a towel by the door your dog uses to come in from the yard. That way, you can wipe his mouth as he comes in with dirt stuck to his lips and before he can rub it against your clothes or shake it all over the walls.

- Keep a bath-sized towel by the door on rainy days. When the dog comes in, drape it over him from head to tail, like a horse blanket. Then pat the dog all over. This will absorb much of the water and is more effective that trying to "wipe" the dog dry by rubbing. Rubbing seems to rearrange the water, rather than soaking it up. Dogs view the patting as a reward and become eager to have the towel draped over them.

- Keep a towel next to your favorite chair(s) so that you can wipe your dog's mouth when he comes for petting.

- Keep the hair around the dog's feet well trimmed, especially the hair between the pads. This will lessen the problem of wet or muddy feet on carpets and floors.

- A soft sponge works really well for brushing hair from clothing and furniture. It is most effective when dampened and well wrung out.

Gentle Bear Laura Ashley, bred by Anne Rogers and owned by Ms. S. Cleeve. Photo by breeder.

Areas of the country that harbor mosquitoes also harbor heartworm. As the name implies, this is not an intestinal parasite; instead the worms grow in the heart until they interfere with heart function and circulation. Mosquitoes spread the infestation, injecting tiny microfilariae into the dog's bloodstream when they bite. It may take months before the dog has a buildup of actual worms in the heart. By this time, the process of eradicating the worms becomes a delicate procedure. It is far safer to use preventive measures. Prevention is provided by monthly doses of a medication which kills the microfilariae before they hatch and become worms. Your veterinarian will probably suggest periodic blood tests to make certain the dog is not infected and then prescribe one of the preventives.

GROOMING YOUR NEWFOUNDLAND

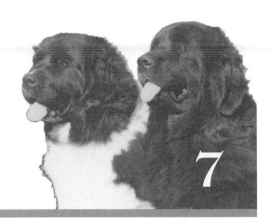

FOR HEALTH AND BEAUTY

7

THE NEWFOUNDLAND HAS A DOUBLE COAT with a longish, somewhat coarse outer coat and a dense, soft undercoat. The undercoat protects the dog against cold air and water, functioning much the same way as down on waterfowl. The undercoat sheds a bit all year round, so grooming is a necessity for the dog's comfort and health. The undercoat will mat if enough loose hair accumulates, leaving the skin unexposed to air. This contributes to skin problems. This is easily kept under control with a weekly deep brushing. Once a year a Newf will shed profusely. For most, this occurs in the spring, but nature is not always consistent and some dogs do not shed until late fall. In addition to their annual shed, bitches, especially younger ones, often shed before they come in season.

A well-groomed dog is not only a pleasure to look at, but it is also important for the owner who wants to keep clothes, home, and car relatively free of dog hair. An added bonus with regular grooming is that you will give your vacuum cleaner and your budget a break. It is amazing how fast a vacuum bag can fill up with dog hair. Grooming a Newfoundland includes brushing, trimming excess hair from ears and feet, cleaning ears,

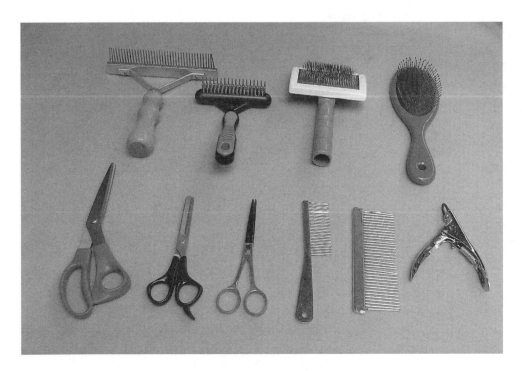

Grooming tools. Top Row: rake, double row rake, slicker brush, pin brush. Bottom Row: shears, thinning shears, curved shears, fine comb, coarse comb, nail trimmers.

trimming nails, and scaling teeth. Brush your Newfie on a weekly basis, and perform other grooming chores as needed.

Minimum grooming tools include a rake, preferably one with two rows of teeth, a slicker brush, a pin brush, a straight-edged shears with rounded tips, thinning shears, nail clippers, a metal dog comb, and a spray bottle with a misting nozzle. All of these may be purchased at pet supply stores, but you can find better, less expensive thinning shears at a beauty supply store.

Training your Newfoundland to stand or lie on a sturdy table so you can work

standing up will make grooming easier. Grooming tables can be purchased at pet supply outlets, but they are a rather expensive item if you have only one dog. A heavy picnic table is both large enough and sturdy enough for a Newf. Use this table outdoors in summer and in a garage or basement during colder weather. As an alternative, if your back and knees don't complain, work on the floor. There is a special feeling of closeness that comes from sitting on the floor with your dog while you work.

BRUSHING AND TRIMMING

The following instructions are for grooming a pet. If you plan to show your Newf, you will need to learn the finer arts of grooming. Regional club members who are successful in showing their dogs are usually happy to help novices. Professional handlers who regularly handle Newfs are also adept at show grooming. They will usually permit their clients to observe and learn from them. It takes a lot of practice to become expert, whether grooming a pet or grooming for show. Fortunately, hair grows back and dogs do not check themselves in the mirror. Your dog will forgive a few mistakes.

First, spray the dog with a fine mist of plain water and work it in well with your hands to prevent hair from flying around during the process. Begin with the rake, removing as much loose hair as possible. The rake works best on the back and sides, moving front to rear and top to bottom with the lay of the hair. Use the slicker or pin brush on the front apron or bib, and to go over areas that were raked. Leg feathering may be brushed with either the pin brush or slicker, and finished with a comb. The pin brush is gentler than a slicker for doing the pantaloons and tail. As you become more adept, depending on the condition of the coat, you will find which tool works best in each area.

When brushing (unlike raking), work from rear to front and from bottom to top.

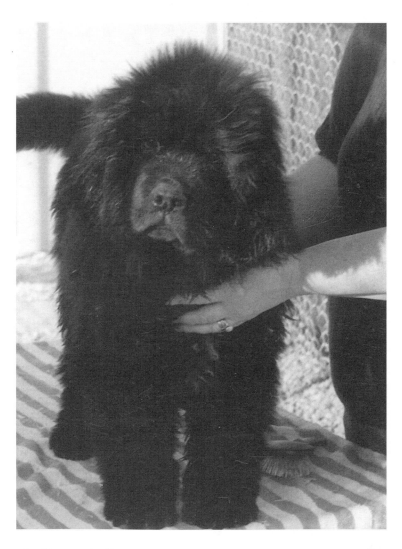

This fifteen-week old *Ironwood* puppy is learning to stand on a grooming table for his weekly grooming. Getting a young puppy accustomed to being groomed will make it an easier and much more pleasant task when he becomes an adult. Photo by Larry Hansen.

This is not to say that you brush against the lay of the hair. Lift the hair in front of the slicker brush with the left hand while the brush goes through the underlayer of hair in the direction of growth. Brush one layer, move the left hand forward to release another layer, and continue brushing. To do the back, begin at the base of the tail. To do legs, ribs, and chest, begin at the lowest point and work up. While the dog is shedding, you may need to brush each area a number of times to remove all the dead hair. Do the longer hair on tail, pantaloons, and feathers the same way, working upward. After brushing the feathers on the legs, run a comb through them as a finishing touch.

Many dogs that otherwise enjoy being brushed do not find it pleasant to have the pantaloons done. Be especially careful in the area of the genitals so your dog will not have reason to resist having the pantaloons groomed. The wire teeth of a slicker brush can cause injury or great discomfort in this delicate area, so, a pin brush is safer. Beauty supply stores have pin brush-type brushes with teeth tipped with small plastic balls. These are ideal for delicate areas. It is best to cover the testicles or vulva with one hand while brushing near them.

Ears and feet are trimmed for neatness. Frequency depends on the owner's tastes and how fast your dog's hair grows. Trim the ear by cutting along the edge of the earflap with the straight-edged shears. Then use thinning shears to shorten the hair on the flap itself. Trim by moving the thinning shears from the tip of the ear toward the skull while snipping rapidly. Remove only a small amount of hair with each snip. Repeat this process a number of times to thin the hair on top of the entire ear. It takes a bit of practice, but after a few haircuts you will become quite proficient.

Trim the feet by using the straight-edged shears to trace the outline of the foot and trim the hair between the pads. Left to grow, this hair will cover the pads and reduce the dog's traction on slippery surfaces. Long hair also collects mud and dust. Snow

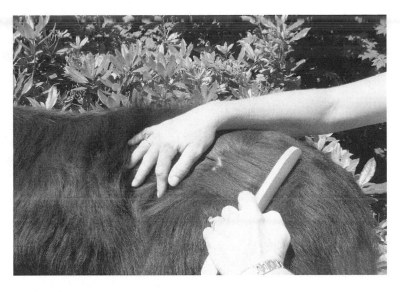

Ingrid Lyden demonstrates how to push the hair forward while brushing, allowing the brush to get down to the skin.

To trim ears, first trim edges with a straight-edged scissors. Then thin hair on ears by clipping with thinning shears moving from bottom to top as shown.

clings to it and forms snowballs. The long hair on the upper foot is also trimmed. Brush or comb it straight up, then use the shears to shorten it.

The dog can be made tidier by thinning the ruff that grows on the chest and up under the jaw.

Use the straight-edged shears by cutting upward through the ruff in front. Then repeat with the long hair over the shoulders and up under the ears.

Use curved shears to shorten hair that has been brushed up. This can be done from the front, but for purposes of the picture, Ingrid approached the foot from behind.

To trim the neck, use a straight-edged shears to cut straight up. Do this several times, then brush out loosened hair. Repeat on the neck area under ears and chin.

Some mats can be removed simply by pulling them apart. Begin with the hair on the edge of the mat and pull a few hairs at a time. Brush with the slicker brush after the hairs are separated. Larger, thicker mats can sometimes be pulled apart if the outside edge is first cut straight across. Then proceed as before.

Some coats tend to mat more readily than others. The most difficult mats to remove are those that cover a wide area and those where the hair is matted down to the skin. Take special care when cutting this kind of mat. It can seem as if you are cutting hair when you are actually cutting the skin. Always work in very good light, use small scissors, and proceed very slowly. Cut only a few hairs at a time, as far from the skin as possible. This will release a small section of the mat. Lift this section so you can see what you are cutting and snip a few more hairs. If it becomes difficult to see what you will be cutting, approach the mat from another side. Occasionally you will need to cut from all sides of a mat before the central hairs will be free enough so you can finally remove the entire mat without cutting the skin. The area under and behind the ears is where Newfs tend to form mats. Take great care removing these mats because the skin around the ear is thin and easily cut. As with most problems, prevention is preferable to a cure. A thorough weekly brushing will all but eliminate a buildup of mats. Brushing also keeps the coat clean.

BATHING

Unless a Newf is being shown, it is not necessary to bathe him regularly. One or two baths a year are sufficient for a Newf that is kept indoors and receives a weekly brushing. Healthy coats have a pleasant odor. A few Newfs manage to keep the hair under the chin damp and begin to smell like a sour towel. Avoid this by keeping the hair short. If your dog has an unpleasant odor and the hair on his back appears oily, it may

Before trimming, Nakiska's Judge Willoughby, owned by the author, appears shaggy and unkept.

After Willy's ears and neck have been thinned and trimmed, he has a much tidier appearance.

This puppy is small enough to fit in a kitchen sink. Note how well the shampoo has been worked into the coat. Photo by Judith Strom.

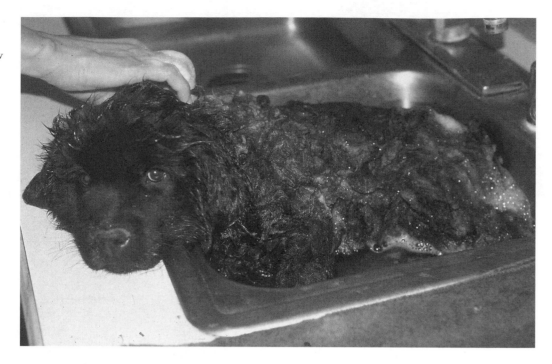

be due to seborrhea. A bath will not eliminate this problem; the condition should be treated by a vet.

Do a thorough grooming before bathing. Remove mats and trim feet and ears. Brush out all loose hair. It may seem as if it would be more pleasant to groom after the dog is clean, but, unfortunately, bathing causes dead hair to mat and makes brushing out the coat very difficult. Another brushing is the final step after a bath, once the dog is dry, or nearly dry. It also gives the coat a finished appearance.

There is a bewildering array of coat care products available for dogs. For general care, shampoo is the only necessity. While any mild shampoo will clean the coat, dog shampoos are worth the extra cost. Dog hair has a different ph balance from that of human hair, and canine shampoos are formulated to compensate for this difference. You may wish to choose a product designed specifically to highlight black coats. Select one that does not contain dyes or coloring agents.

It is easiest to bathe a Newf outdoors; however, bathe him indoors if the temperature outside is below fifty degrees. Do it yourself dog washing facilities area available in many cities and are a good winter alternative if you do not have a suitable area to bathe your Newf indoors at your home. Dog grooming parlors, some veterinary clinics, and boarding kennels with groomers on staff are an alternative to doing it yourself, but this can be costly for a giant breed.

If possible, connect a hose to a sink or laundry tub with warm water. Cold water can be used but is far less effective in penetrating a Newf's oily coat. Find a location where your hose will reach and the dog can be tied safely. Prepare everything before securing the dog. Attach a trigger spray nozzle to the hose and adjust the water temperature. Most dog shampoos come in squeeze bottles they will not spill if tipped over. Have the shampoo ready. Finally, attach the dog to his lead and tether him.

Wet the dog as thoroughly as possible with warm water, then apply shampoo. You will find that as the shampoo is applied, you will be able to wet areas that repelled water during the initial spraying. Spray the shampooed area with the hose again, and apply more shampoo. When the dog is thoroughly wet and covered with shampoo, rub into a lather and work the shampoo down to the skin.

When using the spray near the ear, grasp the ear at its base and hold it shut so that water will not go inside. The face should not be shampooed or sprayed, but can be cleaned with a damp cloth.

Rinse carefully and thoroughly. Soap residue causes itching and irritation. Some groomers like to use diluted vinegar as a final rinse. Release the dog to shake. In warm weather he can be left to dry outdoors. Bring him inside in cooler weather. Newfs can be bathed outdoors in weather as cool as fifty degrees, but should not be left out longer than necessary to shake off excess water. This breed will swim in icy water with no ill effects because the natural oil in the coat prevents the water from coming in contact with the skin. Bathing temporarily removes the oil. A coat wet to the skin may cause the dog to become chilled.

TRIMMING NAILS

Nail trimming, like all grooming procedures, should begin in puppyhood. Long nails cause discomfort and poor traction on slippery surfaces. They can also distort the feet. Dogs do not like having their feet handled and are especially wary when their nails are involved. Handle a puppy's feet whenever you pet him so that he gets used to being touched in that area. If the puppy is not manageable on your lap, get someone to help distract him while you concentrate on trimming the nails. An unwilling dog the size of an adult Newf can make the task of nail trimming almost impossible. If you have no experience in trimming nails and your adult dog has not been well trained to accept this procedure, it is advisable to have a professional groomer or veterinary assistant cut his nails the first time. Watch the process and ask questions so you can learn to do it yourself.

The main concern when trimming nails is to avoid cutting the quick, or center area of the nail where blood circulates. Cutting

the quick causes the dog pain and the nail to bleed. A product to stop bleeding, available at pet supply stores, should be kept with your nail trimmer in case you need it.

If your Newf has white feet, his nails may be translucent. The quick will appear as a pinkish "tube" inside the nail, making it easier to cut the nail safely without touching the quick. Unfortunately, the quick cannot be seen through the black outer layer on the nails of most Newfs. For this reason, take only thin slices of the nail with each cut. The inside of the nail is grayish-white in color. The quick appears as a blackish spot in the center. As you pare off thin layers, you will see this spot appear before you cut into it. As soon as you see it, stop trimming. If the dog's nails are still too long, wait a week to trim them again. The quick will have receded slightly during this time.

Obviously, it is best not to let the nails become overgrown, but if it

Two types of commonly used nail clippers.

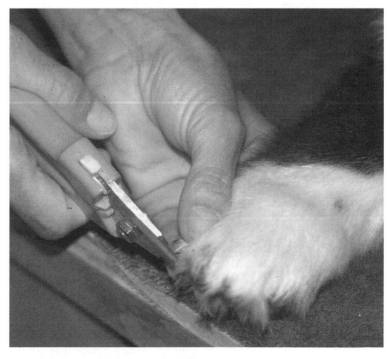

Teach your dog to lie quietly at the edge of the table while your trim his front feet. He can be placed on his side while you trim the back feet, or you can hold the foot up while he is standing. Photo by Judith Strom.

Ch. *Ursula's* Black Gold is beautifully groomed and ready to be shown. She is owned by her breeder. Photo by Astrid Indreboe.

happens, be patient. It is better to take off a little of the excess once a week than to cut into the quick. Even the most cooperative dog will become reluctant to have his nails worked on once this happens.

OTHER ROUTINE GROOMING

The Newf is a drop-eared breed, as opposed to breeds with erect ears. Drop ears prevent air from getting into the ear and need more frequent attention and cleaning than erect ears. Commercial products for ear cleaning are available from your vet or pet supply. Follow the instructions for putting the solution into the ear, then with your fingers, mas-

sage the outer base of the ear to work the solution around and loosen the debris. As soon as you let go, your dog will probably give a vigorous shake, sending the fluid in all directions. Next you should swab the ear with a cotton ball or swab. Get into the nooks and crannies but don't penetrate too deeply into the ear canal. Never probe farther into the ear than you can see. A weekly check will show whether there is an accumulation of waxy substance. If there is a "cheesy" odor or rapid buildup of exudate, have the ears checked by the vet. Your dog could have ear mites or an infection of the ear canal that could lead to deafness and other problems.

Cleaning the teeth prevents tartar buildup, helps keep teeth and gums healthy,

Int'l Norwegian, Swedish, Danish Ch. *Birkorella's* Octavia Itchitouch with her tiny "mistress," owned by Rigmor and Anne-Katherine Ulstad. Photo by co-breeder, Astrid Indreboe.

and should begin in puppyhood. It is advisable to observe the process before attempting it. Your vet or a dog groomer can show you how it is done. You can use a tooth scaler or a number of different types of brushes and cleaners that are now available for regular cleaning. If tartar builds up despite your best efforts, have your dog's teeth cleaned at the vet clinic. Tartar buildup contributes to infections and heart problems, especially in older dogs.

The Newfoundland is not an "easy care" breed when it comes to grooming, However, neither do Newfies need daily maintenance. Weekly grooming is the ideal, rather than a rigid necessity. Your Newf will not become a hopeless mess if he misses a grooming session now and then.

If you approach grooming with the dog's comfort in mind so that he learns to enjoy it, grooming becomes a bonding experience between dog and owner—one that many Newf owners would not trade.

Newfoundlands enjoy any type of activity having to do with water.

ACTIVITIES TO ENJOY

JUST FOR FUN

8

STUDIES SHOW THAT DOG OWNERS TEND TO be healthier than non-dog owners, presumably because dogs keep people active. Dogs are much more rewarding to their owners, emotionally as well as physically, when sharing activities. Play is the first activity that comes to mind and one of the first things one does with a new puppy. Except in the smallest yards, it is possible to play catch and retrieve, hide and seek, or invent games together.

Walking the dog is probably the next most common activity. We are amazed to see how many people walk past our house now compared to ten years ago. More amazing is the number of walkers who have their dogs on lead with them. I would guess that there are more walkers with dogs than without. I doubt there are many dog walkers who would not agree that it is far more interesting to exercise with a dog. Dogs, like small children, have great enthusiasm, even for what appears mundane to us. Both dogs and kids help to heighten awareness of our surroundings and make them more interesting.

Newfies add yet another dimension. Their size, coupled with their benign and gentle demeanor, attracts the attention of other walkers, children, and neighbors. Walking with a Newf inevitably results in social connections. Sometimes the encounters are simply exchanges of smiles or greetings. Others end in longer conversations and occasionally in lasting friendships.

It is important to make your dog welcome in parks and neighborhoods by making sure he is a good citizen. He should not trespass on anyone's property. He should not approach anyone who does not invite an approach. Males should not be allowed to lift their legs on shrubs, flowers, car tires, or other personal property. Every owner should carry a plastic bag for picking up any "deposits" the

N. Clarke walks with his dog. *Bearcove* Coastguard pulls a cart, and Toy Poodle, Minty, pulls his own little cart. Photo by Anne Rogers.

dog makes along the way. All this requires is slipping your hand inside the bag, picking up the deposit and then turning the bag inside out. You may want to take a second bag, plastic or paper, to put the first one into for aesthetic reasons. (Considering their size, it is especially essential to clean up after your Newf to maintain good relations with others and to keep dogs welcome in the community.)

HUNTING

Newfoundlands are natural retrievers and can be used for duck hunting. Most are "soft mouthed" and will not damage birds brought to shore. Several years ago a woman bought a Newfoundland, with grudging acquiescence from her husband who wanted a sporting breed for duck hunting. The man totally ignored the dog for two years. One fall day, on impulse, he took the dog hunting with him. The Newf watched as the first duck was dropped, noting where it had fallen. He was ordered to retrieve it. Despite the fact that he had never been trained, the dog plunged into the water, but returned to shore without the bird. In disgust the man watched the Newf leave the water and retreat to a high bank above the shore. Then, to his amazement, he saw the dog dive from the bank back into the water, swim directly to the duck and return it to shore. From that day on, that Newf had two devoted owners instead of one.

HIKING AND PACKING

With an increased number of people enjoying wilderness camping and hiking, Newf owners are learning the pleasure and value of their pets as trail companions. Newfs can carry backpacks that are large enough to be of some use to the hiker. For a trek of several days, the dog can carry his own food and water. For day hikes he can carry extra clothes and light gear for the

hiker. Never consider a dog a "pack mule." A dog's back structure is different from traditional pack animals and can be injured by heavy loads. The most important reasons for hiking with a dog are companionship and offering an enhanced set of senses.

In wildlands, it is essential that dogs be trained in trail, camp, and wilderness manners so they will not be a nuisance or hazard to wildlife, the environment, other hikers, or their owner. Dogs must be taught to stay beside the hiker whether off or on lead. If he cannot be trusted off lead, the lead should stay on. Dogs may not chase wildlife or approach other hikers uninvited. They should not be allowed to enter any body of water without the hiker's permission. Just as with humans, dogs should not eliminate near any pond, lake, or stream where the waste could seep into the water.

One great pleasure of hiking with a trained dog is the relationship achieved between dog and owner. Dogs show the same enthusiasm when hiking in the wilderness as they do when walking in the neighborhood, but their senses are of even greater value in this environment, which is less hospitable to humans than their home turf. Sensitive owners notice that due to the dog's acute senses, his behavior increases their own awareness. Dogs detect the presence of other humans or animals before the hiker is aware of them. Their senses can alert the hiker to unseen dangers such as a fire, landslide, or an impending storm. Due to their unique scenting ability, dogs are capable of helping a lost hiker find his trail. However, do not expect your dog to be a reliable partner until both you and your dog have spent many, many hours together on the trail. It takes a long time for hiker and dog to learn to read each other and communicate in this environment.

EXERCISING IN DOG PARKS

Exercise areas for dogs are available in some cities. These are usually areas fenced

Ethan and Golly were among several generations of Newfs trained as pack dogs. They carried their own food, water, and light gear, all of which rarely totaled as much as twenty pounds. The Newfs were accepted as partners, who, through their special sensitivities, could add to the experience of wilderness travel and, to some extent, could serve as protection.

Both dogs became very useful at finding the trail. Although they had been trained in wilderness manners and safety, they required no training in trail finding. It was under circumstances of need that each dog first demonstrated this ability. Their owner was used to hiking off trail or following animal paths that crisscrossed one another. On the return trip he was sometimes uncertain which trail would lead back. One late afternoon in winter he found himself in such a situation. The remaining daylight did not allow time for trial and error and although equipped, he was not anxious to spend an unplanned night in the woods.

He said to his dog, "Golly, find the trail," and motioned for the dog to go ahead. Golly, trained to walk behind his owner, went ahead a few steps on one of the paths. Then he paused, looked over his shoulder, and waited for his partner to take the lead. The trail he had selected led back to the car.

Ethan, who came several generations after Golly, demonstrated his ability under similar circumstances. He not only could find the way back, but also could find the way to a certain destination in situations where a trail had long been abandoned and visual clues were insufficient for a human to follow. It is not remarkable that the dogs, with their acute of smell, could find the right trails. What is remarkable is the Newfoundland's ability to understand a need and respond to it appropriately.

Alan Riley hiking in the Cascades with *Seamount* Whaleboat Teddy. Teddy, a trained pack dog and trail companion, was bred by the author and trained by Alan. Photo by author.

Yeti *vom Schwarzen Baeren* tows Marina Froehlich in water practice. Marina's dogs, Yeti and Emerson, go to work with her every day. In Austria, dogs are allowed almost everywhere, including restaurants and street-cars. Photo by Arno Froehlich.

off in a public park. They provide an excellent opportunity for doggy exercise as well as the canine socialization that "single" dogs miss. It is up to owners to watch their dogs after turning them loose with other dogs. Usually the scene is one of peaceful chaos, with dogs chasing, feinting, somersaulting, and mounting each other. Without human interference, dogs off lead usually seem to work out the dominance order without undue threats, growling, or fighting.

There are some risks in putting a dog into such an area. One risk is exposure to disease. Owners who care enough to go to the trouble of transporting their dogs to these places are also the ones who seek regular veterinary care and immunization. Even so, there is no required proof of vaccination, and there is no immunization against parasites such as fleas, various worms, and fungal infections that other dogs may carry. Rough play can result in sprains, strains, and more severe injuries. An undiagnosed orthopedic problem may be exacerbated by hard play. Make sure your dog is in good physical condition. Most dogs know the canine rules for social interaction, but owners must be prepared to break up occasional fights.

SWIMMING

Swimming is wonderful exercise for both Newfs and their owners. Beaches established for humans do not usually allow dogs, but there are non-beach areas where you can take your dog to swim. If the water is too cold for you, it will not affect your dog. His undercoat, which is almost waterproof, will allow him to enjoy cold water without your company. He can be encouraged to plunge in to retrieve anything he can hold in his mouth that will not sink. (Some dogs will duck for submerged objects and other will actually dive for them.)

Be sure that your dog will come when called before you let him go. Some dogs are so carried away with swimming that they will continue far out in the water beyond reach of their owner's voices. Boat skippers or water ski riders may not see a swimming dog. Other hazards are areas with weeds that can entangle a dog.

I once rescued one of our Newfs under circumstances I would never have anticipated. This dog had never been swimming, but when we got close to a marina at a nearby lake, he rushed for the water, pulling the lead out of my grasp. He climbed over the huge rocks brought in for the marina and placed along the shoreline. It took me a few seconds to recover from his sudden bolt and I followed, unable to scramble on two feet over the rocks as neatly as he had done on four. When I finally reached the edge of the rock pile, he was nearly twenty feet away. I called and he immediately turned and swam toward me. However, something was terribly wrong. He began going under water. When he came up, I called again and the same thing happened. In a panic, I plunged in and swam to him; unable to believe my Newf was sinking. I grabbed the lead close to his neck and started for shore but found the lead was caught, perhaps on a rock that had rolled away from those dumped along the shore. I managed to jiggle the lead free and we swam to shore. It took awhile for the whole thing to sink in and become understandable.

Allowing your dog to swim in rivers and streams requires some knowledge and a careful examination of the conditions. The first time we exposed a Newf to running water was when we took our first Newf puppy to the mountains. We stopped by a stream and the puppy waded into the water. Within a very short time we saw our puppy swimming frantically as he was being carried downstream by the current. My husband ran into the water after him, but he soon discovered that he was no match in keeping up with the fast water. Both of us then rushed along the bank until the puppy was carried to a backwater where we were able to catch him. It was a terrifying experience for all of us. This was the foolish behavior of two owners unfamiliar with fast water. Unless you know how to "read" a river and know what is downstream from you, it is reckless to let your dog go into the water. Obvious hazards are rapids or waterfalls, large or small. Snags are extremely dangerous. A snag is a tree that has fallen into the water and remains in place, held by roots or branches. Even the best swimmers, dog or human, are helpless against snags because they "hold" the swimmer while the current pulls him under.

OBEDIENCE TRAINING

Training is a crucial activity for dog and owner. Humane shelters state that behavior problems are the most frequently cited reasons for owners to relinquish their pets. Unless one has already trained a dog, it is most productive to attend obedience classes. Obedience classes, led by an instructor and an assistant, teach the owner to train the dog. The advantage of classes, other than having expert help, is that the dog learns to be with other dogs and people and he learns to work amid distractions. Not only does the dog learn the basic manners he will need for a lifetime, but he and the owner bond through the training in class and at home between classes. If both dog and owner take to obedience work, there are advanced classes that can keep this activity going over several years.

The American Kennel Club has established a system for testing dogs for the Canine Good Citizen (CGC) award. This is not a title conferred by the AKC, but rather a certificate to show that a dog has passed certain requirements. Testing occurs in many areas and testers can be found through obedience clubs and 4-H groups. The AKC website offers detailed information on the exercises and how to have your dog tested for a certificate. Some of the criteria include accepting a friendly stranger, sitting politely for petting, walking through a crowd, and staying on command.

THERAPY WORK

Newfs are wonderful as therapy dogs. Therapy dogs visit nursing homes, children's hospitals, and other institutions where patients welcome the comfort and the special kind of communication that dogs bring. Some adults and children, who have been

Bearbrook's Rufus works as a therapy dog and has a popular following at the nursing home where he is a regular visitor. He earned special state certification for pet therapy. Photo by owner, Karen Steinrock.

unable to respond to humans, have responded to dogs by hugging, petting, and even speaking to them. Newfs, with their sensitive natures and love for people, are naturals for this activity. Some obedience clubs contact nursing homes and children's hospitals to organize scheduled visits with volunteer handlers and dogs. Other individual dog owners make the contacts themselves and set their own schedules. Some institutions require that visiting dogs are "Canine Good Citizens."

A later chapter will further describe obedience and other competitive activities for you and your Newf.

Some residents from the nursing home attended the National Specialty show to watch Rufus and other Newfs compete. Photo by Michael Bupp, courtesy of *The Sentinel,* Carlisle, PA.

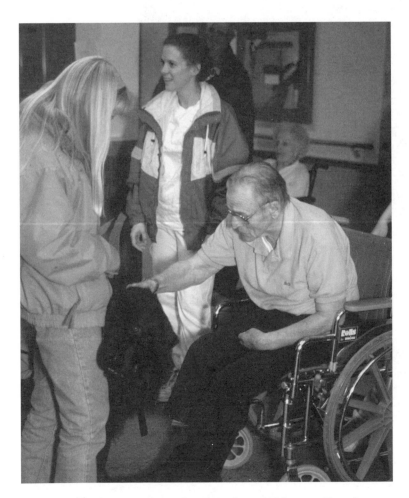

A Newfoundland visits residents of a nursing home in Montana. Photo by Judith Strom.

VN Ch. *Tatoosh's* Huggable Nakiska, ROM, and VN *Nakiska's* Nitro Punch. The gear is appropriate— both dogs have numerous Water Test titles. Photo by Ingrid Lyden.

ACTIVITIES AND COMPETITIONS

PROVE YOUR DOG'S ABILITY

9

THE AMERICAN KENNEL CLUB CLASSIFIES the Newfoundland as a member of the Working Group. His tasks in the past have included pulling carts and sleds, carrying backpacks, and helping the fishermen of Newfoundland pull in their heavy nets. These were jobs requiring strength, endurance, and patience—the same traits evident in our present-day Newfs.

Newfoundland owners enjoy bringing out the working abilities of their dogs in recreational and competitive activities. The Newfoundland Club of America established a Working Dog Committee to help maintain and promote these abilities. This committee has developed a series of exercises and rules for Water Tests and for Draft competitions, and has developed and revised manuals that provide assistance in training Newfs for this work.

WATER TESTS

Water competitions had been held in the United States as early as 1929, but the the first test at which the Newfoundland Club of America awarded Water Dog and Water Rescue Dog title certificates was in July 1973 at Horton, Michigan. Three dogs passed the Junior Division exercises and one also passed the Senior Division exercises the same day.

Ch. *CastaNewf's* So To Speak swam out with Denise and is now towing her back as part of the Junior Division Water Test. Sunny, bred and owned by Denise Castonguay, has numerous Championship, Working, and Water Test Titles. Photo by Pam Mohr.

VN Ch. *Nakiska's* Spellbound dives to retrieve a paddle tossed into the water in the Senior Division Water Test. She will return it to her owner and handler, Lanelle Warrick. Photo by Julie Saunders.

Since that day, Water Tests have been held each year in different regions, making it possible for Newfs to earn the titles of Water Dog (WD) and Water Rescue Dog (WRD). To earn a Water title in either division, a dog must pass all exercises at a single test.

The WD is a Junior Division title awarded to Newfs passing exercises that include, among others: retrieving a boat bumper thrown from shore, retrieving a life jacket or boat cushion dropped from a boat, and carrying a line to a steward standing or treading water about fifty feet from shore. These exercises are the basics that prepare a dog for the Senior Division exercises, which are more complex and more applicable to water rescue situations.

Senior Division Exercises lead to the WRD title. Included are diving from a boat to retrieve a canoe paddle, taking a line to a steward in a boat and towing the boat to shore, and taking a life ring to one of three stewards about seventy-five feet from shore. The judge tells the handler which steward is to be "rescued" and the handler directs the dog to that steward. The dog tows the steward to shore. The dog also must drive off a boat to "rescue" his handler who "falls" from

the boat. The dog must swim to the handler and tow him to shore.

Plans are underway to introduce a new level of testing, the Water Rescue Dog Excellent (WRDX) test. In this exercise, the dog will see a boat capsize and must swim out to rescue the "victim" from under the boat and return him or her to shore.

Achieving a water rescue title takes many hours of training and practice. Although the exercises are based upon the Newf's natural instincts, standards of performance are rigorous and must be met completely in order for the dog to pass. Regulations and exercises for the Water Tests are available from the NCA.

CARTING AND DRAFT DOG COMPETITIONS

The dog cart, once a symbol of canine labor, is now a symbol of pleasure for Newfs and their young passengers. Most Newfs love to pull and, when they become used to the rattling and bumping of a cart behind them, look forward to being hitched up. Some Newfs take to the cart the first time they are put in the traces.

The Newfoundland Club of America offers Draft Tests, leading to the title Draft Dog (DD). These are often held in conjunction with Water Tests. The dogs pull their carts through a series of exercises to demonstrate their abilities to respond to commands and maneuver successfully through a pattern. Exercises include starting, stopping, right and left turns, and backing.

Proper balance, light weight, and wheels that move easily are important factors in selecting a dog cart. A comfortable harness and hitching arrangement is also important. The *Draft Equipment Guide* available from the Newfoundland Club of America includes charts, patterns, and guides for making equipment, sources for ready-made equipment, and guidelines for working with draft dogs.

A carting competition is held each year at the National Specialty show. Carts are decorated and handlers costumed around the theme of the show. Carts include an interesting variety of two- and four-wheeled carts, and even an occasional travois, some of which have been transported across the country for the event. Along with the clever decorations and costumes, the opportunity to watch Newfs perform a traditional task makes the carting competition a popular spectator attraction.

A few Newfoundlands can be seen competing in dog pulls, where the dog that pulls the heaviest load in his weight division wins. However, Newfoundlands were not bred to pull such excessively heavy loads (2000 pounds or more) and I do not recommend this as a suitable activity for the breed.

OBEDIENCE

Young Newfoundlands exhibit the same exuberance as the youngsters of less-placid breeds, but the size and weight of a Newfie pup make early training more important than for a smaller breed. Most obedience groups accept puppies into their classes at

VN Am. Can. Ch. *Cameroon* Captain Midnight, with owner Lanelle Warrick, takes part in a draft test. The dog has several Working and Water Test titles. Photo by Judi Adler.

Mike Lovett leads "Micky Mouse" at a Decorative Carting Competition at a National Specialty show. Photo by Sandee Lovett.

six months of age. Some hold "Kindergarten Puppy Training" (KPT) classes for younger puppies, which are a kind of canine preschool. It is an advantage to both puppy and owner to attend such a session if a puppy's age qualifies him at the time classes begin. If you cannot take your dog to a

Betty McDonnell practices the heel off-lead exercise with VN Ch. *Kilyka's* Every Amenity. "Amy" has several Obedience and Working titles and has twice been High Scoring Newf at National Specialty shows. Photo by George McDonnell.

Newfoundland *Sweetbay's* Boudicca, UD, checks out articles in scent discrimination. Photo © Judith E. Strom.

puppy class, enroll him in a regular obedience class as soon as possible after he reaches the minimum age.

Basic obedience instructs you to teach the dog to heel, sit, stay, lie down, stand still, and come. Some people have a natural ability to train dogs and can teach their dogs the basic commands without help. However, there is still an advantage in attending a class. The dogs learn to behave amid the distractions of other dogs and people and to obey away from familiar surroundings. The training methods have been honed to a high degree of efficiency and serve as a basis for further training.

If you plan to attend an obedience class, check the credentials of the trainer or trainers. Most large urban areas have obedience training clubs (with non-profit status) that offer classes. The unpaid clubs' trainers are qualified by experience in training their own dogs and through apprenticeship programs with other trainers.

You also can find excellent trainers who hold private classes. When checking the trainer's credentials, ask how many dogs he or she has trained to AKC obedience titles. The answer should be more than one or two. Also, ask for the names of dog owners who have participated in the trainer's classes. You may wish to inquire as to their satisfaction with the training sessions. If you find a trainer with experience in working with your breed, so much the better.

Newfoundlands have a desire to please and are pleasant dogs to work with in obedience. It is easy to be caught up in obedience training as a sport. If you find the work satisfying and enjoy the social activity of training with others, you may want to compete to earn AKC obedience titles.

Obedience Trials are held at most all-breed dog shows, and there are three levels of competition: *Novice, Open,* and *Utility. Novice* is for dogs that have completed beginning obedience and are working toward the Companion Dog (CD) title. Exercises in Novice include heeling on and off leash, standing to be examined, coming on command, sitting

VN Ch. Klykus Daddy's Dakota Sport, owned by Lori and Stan Peznowski, does a retrieve over high jump in Open obedience class. Photo by Garry Baldwin.

for one minute, and lying down for three minutes with the handler across the ring from the dog. *Open* competition is for dogs that have completed the second stage of training. The work includes drop on recall, retrieving a dumbbell on the flat, retrieving over the high jump, broad jump, long sit with handler out of sight for three minutes, and long down with handler out of sight for five minutes. These dogs are working toward the Companion Dog Excellent (CDX) title. *Utility* is the highest level and includes signal exercise, scent discrimination, directed retrieve, directed jumping, and a moving stand. Dogs in this class are working toward the Utility Dog (UD) title.

At each level of obedience work, dogs must earn at least 170 out of 200 points in three separate trials in order to earn a title for that level. Obedience may be enjoyed as a competitive sport in which a handler and his dog vie with others for high scores and one of four placement ribbons awarded in each class, or a handler may choose to compete for the sense of achievement from eventually earning a title or titles for his or her Newf. Handlers with highly competitive

Sweetbay's Boudicca, UD, working on hand signals in the Utility class. Photo © Judith E. Strom.

dogs that achieve high scores may set their sights on earning points toward the highly esteemed Obedience Trial Championship (OTCh.)

Kiredor's The Mighty Quinn, owned by Dejah and Steve Petsch, takes a broad jump. "Quinner" has Obedience and Water Test titles and is working toward an Agility title. Photo by Temple Imaging Services.

TRACKING

Tracking Dog (TD) titles may also be earned. In tracking exercises the dog demonstrates his ability to follow human scent on a course laid out before the test. The track must be at least a half-hour old before the first dog is tested. Weather, lay of the land, ground cover, and wind vary from test to test. In order to pass, the dog must be able to adjust to whatever conditions are present at the test site where he is working. He must follow the path of the tracklayer and find articles dropped by that person. The Tracking Dog Excellent (TDX) test is more advanced, with a track that is at least three hours old. Unlike Obedience, which requires passing scores in three trials, Tracking requires a single passing score.

AGILITY

Agility is the most recent competitive event. The competition began in England as an entertaining event based on equine show jumping competition. It soon caught on and interest spread rapidly throughout the world. Dogs run at full speed with their handlers beside them. The dogs maneuver through, over, and under a series of props such as walking up and down a teeter-totter, running through a fabricated tunnel, jumping through a suspended ring, climbing a A-frame, and zigzagging through a row of weave poles. Timing, as well as speed and competence, is involved in this exciting sport. As in Obedience, a new title is conferred when a dog has passed the required trials at each higher level of difficulty.

Cedar Pond's Jesse, who has Obedience, Working, and Water Test titles, tackles a dog walk in an Agility competition. Jesse is owned by Chuck Lalungo. Photo by Mark Sturtz.

VN Am. Can. Ch. *Seabrook's* Belladonna Delmar emerges from the tunnel in a Versatility competition. Among other honors, "Babe" was the Number One Newfoundland in Novice Agility at over seven years of age. She is owned by Lawren Kinney. Photo by Woof Studios.

"Babe" approaches the end of the weave poles in Agility. Photo by Woof Studios.

Sweetbay's Bosco TDX, NA, sails through the tire jump. Photo © Judith E. Strom.

Bosco navigates the teeter totter. The dog must touch the yellow "contact zone" when descending from the obstacle. Photo © Judith E. Strom.

Agility is a high-energy sport and the dogs love it. It has become a popular spectator sport at many dog shows. Part of the enjoyment comes from seeing the excitement and enthusiasm of the dogs while performing. There are numerous levels and types of agility competitions. They are held in conjunction with AKC shows and also hosted as separate events by a number of organizations. Check the organizations listed in Other Sources of Information for current rules, regulations, and other information.

If you want to become involved in this lively sport, locate a training center in your locality that gives classes. Because of the jumping aspect, it is best to wait until your Newf is at least eighteen months of age to begin serious training, but puppies will enjoy many of the non-jumping exercises and may be introduced to these in puppy kindergarten class.

CONFORMATION SHOWS

Showing dogs in conformation (or breed) classes has become increasingly popular as a sport. Nevertheless, dog shows have a serious aspect as well. The show ring largely determines the future of each breed. It is an arena where breeders and exhibitors demonstrate and test the success of their breeding programs. Consistent winners are in demand as stud dogs. Puppies from top winning bitches are sought after. These animals' genes become widely disseminated and affect future generations. A judge holds an awesome responsibility when making a selection.

It is thought that the first championship title awarded to a Newfoundland in the United States was given to a dog named Sam in 1883. AKC records show that the first Championship Certificate was awarded to Major II in 1913. It was not until the late 1960s and early 1970s that Newfs could be found at most large dog shows. Even today, Newf entries do not compare with those of more popular breeds, yet quite a number finish their championships each year.

Dog show judges are approved by the American Kennel Club to judge specific breeds. When judging, they try to determine which dog and bitch, according to the breed Standard, are the best representatives of their breed. To do this, a judge examines each entry by looking at the overall outline of the dog and by feeling the dog's structure. Each entry is gaited to show his movement from the front, rear, and side.

Shows offer six classes for dogs and six classes for bitches in each breed. Specialty shows for Newfoundlands may offer additional classes. The winner of each class competes against the winners of the same sex from the other classes for Winners Dog or Winners Bitch awards. Winners Dog and Winners Bitch compete with any champions in their breed for Best of Breed and Best of Opposite Sex. They also compete against each other for Best of Winners. The Newfoundland awarded Best of Breed competes with other Working Group breed winners for Working Group placements, and the winner of the Working Group goes on to compete against winners of the six other Groups for the Best in Show award.

Both the Winners Dog and Winners Bitch receive points toward a championship title. The number of points won at a given

Ch. *Mooncusser's* Ships in the Nite after his bath at the National Specialty show. His expressionis typical of a Newf being bathed. They are usually stoical, even though they don't much care for the process. Owned by breeder. Photo by Charisse Andrews.

This Landseer is being "baited" with food to get an alert expression for the judge. Photo © Kent and Donna Dannen.

show depends upon the number of dogs competing and the region of the country where they are being shown. Each seven regional divisions have a schedule showing how many dogs must compete in order to win a certain number of points. The number of points that may be earned at a single show ranges from one to five. To earn a championship, a dog must win a total of fifteen points, with major wins under at least two different judges. Three to five points are considered a major win.

The AKC maintains cumulative records of the points a dog has won and automatically awards a Championship Certificate when the requirements have been met. Exhibitors should keep all ribbons and awards from shows where their dogs have placed, and also keep a record of the points their dogs have won in case there is any question about the dog's status.

If you are interested in showing your Newfoundland, whether a puppy or an

Retired Marine Corp Col. Jerry Weiss judges Newfoundlands at the Flatiron Kennel Club show. Photo © Kent and Donna Dannen.

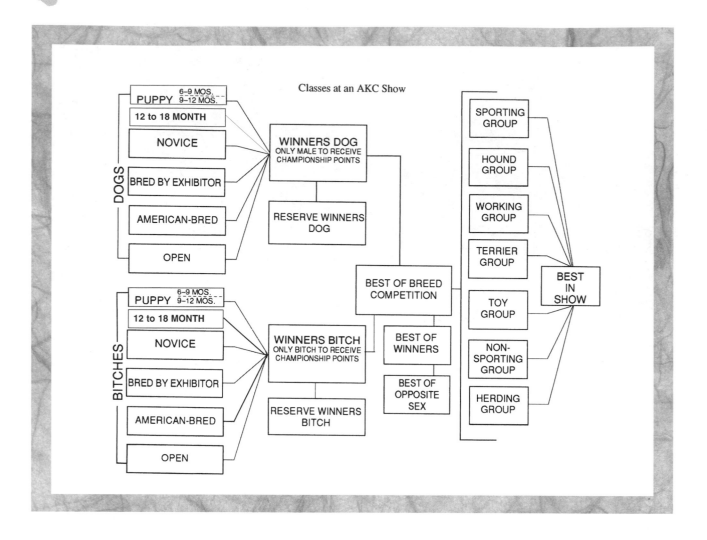

Classes at an AKC Show

adult, have your dog evaluated for his show potential before investing the time and funds required to show him properly. Begin with your dog's breeder, if he or she lives nearby. Ask other Newf fanciers for their opinions. Type, that elusive quality that embodies the essentials of a breed, is extremely important in a show dog. While professional handlers or experts in other breeds may be able to tell you whether your dog is well put together and moves well, it takes someone very familiar with high quality Newfoundlands to tell you whether your dog has the type required to be successful in the show ring.

If you decide to show your Newf, you need to begin learning about shows and showing. Study the breed Standard so you can identify the strengths and weaknesses of your dog. Go to the AKC website for a copy of "Rules Applying to Registration and Dog

Shows." Every dog show exhibitor is responsible for knowing these rules. Attend dog shows and watch the Newfoundlands and other breeds being judged.

Next, you must learn how to train your dog to gait and stand to be examined. In addition, you will need to know how to handle your dog and present him to his best advantage. Grooming for shows requires advanced skills and finesse not required for pet grooming.

If there is a regional Newfoundland club in your area, you will find individuals willing to help you prepare to show your Newf. Some clubs hold handling classes and grooming sessions. Most regional clubs hold annual fun matches. These serve as practice shows for dogs and handlers.

All-breed fun matches also offer an opportunity to practice showing. Information

Manlio Massa of Italy judges a Hungarian bitch at the NCA National Specialty. It is a small world when it comes to Newfoundlands. Photo by Jeff Visotsky.

Josh going Best of Breed at the 2002 Newfoundland National Specialty show, one of three back to back wins at this important venue for Newfoundlands. Bred by Carol Bergman and owned by Peggy Helming. Photo by Ashbey Photography.

on upcoming matches can be found in newspaper want ads or pet columns. Veterinary and pet shop bulletin boards are also sources of information on fun matches.

The best preparation for showing is to attend a handling class. These are offered by breed clubs or professional handlers. You will be trained in gaiting and stacking (posing) your dog, and will learn ring procedure, show protocol, and how to enter shows. Handling classes are often listed in the pet section of newspaper ads, or advertised by trainers. If you cannot find such a listing, try calling boarding and breeding kennels listed in the classified section of the telephone directory. Some of these will be show exhibitors and may know of clubs or individuals offering classes.

The dog fancy is like a communications network. Anyone seeking information or help can find it if he or she is persistent. A call to one individual may not offer the information you need, but chances are excellent that a second or third call will offer referrals to others who can help.

Seasoned exhibitors often wait until a dog is somewhat mature before showing him. For most Newfs, this means waiting until the dog is two years or older. If you are eager to start showing while your dog is a puppy or a yearling, do not be disappointed if he does not make any big wins. Unless a puppy or youngster is truly outstanding or unusually well-developed for his age, he will not be ready to compete against older, more mature dogs for championship points. Consider the first year of showing as experience for you and your dog. If you win occasionally, you will be fortunate. As long as showing is fun, win or lose, and you are convinced that your dog is worthy of being shown, these early ring experience will serve you and your dog well when the time comes for him to take his place in the winners lineup.

Five VNs all bred, owned, and trained by Ingrid and Chris Lyden. All were from the same dam, VN Ch. *Tatoosh's* Huggable Nakiska, ROM. In addition to their VN Ch. titles, together they hold eighteen titles plus two ROM titles. Photo by Kaj Bune.

THE NEWFOUNDLAND CLUB OF AMERICA

THE OFFICIAL "PARENT" CLUB

10

THE AMERICAN KENNEL CLUB (AKC) IS widely recognized in the United States. A new puppy owner will proudly tell friends that his puppy is AKC registered, expecting the friend to be familiar with the term. Probably neither realizes that AKC registration means little more than that the breeder has filed the necessary papers to certify when the puppy was whelped, that the puppy is pure-bred from AKC registered stock, and that the sire, dam, and breeder are those listed on the registration.

Occasionally, a purebred (not thoroughbred, a term which applies to horses) dog owner will inquire about becoming a member of the AKC. It is a common misunderstanding that one can become a member. Actually, the AKC is made up of member clubs, each of which is entitled to send a delegate to represent the club at AKC delegate meetings. Member clubs include obedience clubs, all-breed clubs, and breed specialty clubs that have applied for, and fulfilled, the requirements to become member clubs of the AKC.

The Newfoundland Club of America (NCA) is one such club. It is made up of individual members. Since the NCA was founded in 1930, it has grown to include over twenty-two hundred members, representing twenty-two countries.

The first American Newfoundland Standard, describing the ideal Newfoundland, was approved in 1930 and was simply an adoption of the British Standard. A new Standard was written by an NCA committee and approved by the membership in 1970. A later version was written and approved in 1990.

The NCA's purpose, as stated in the Constitution and By-Laws, is "to encourage and promote the quality of pure-bred Newfoundland dogs and to do all possible to bring their natural qualities to perfection." Its activities and programs demonstrate interest in protecting and improving the breed. Committees working with these concerns include: Health and Longevity, Newfoundland Rescue, Research Advisory, Working Dog, Health Challenge, Obedience, and General Education. The club maintains a Newfoundland database and hosts a web page where anyone interested in the breed can obtain a wealth of information on Newfoundlands, regional clubs, rescue, health concerns, and activities.

The NCA has developed a series of events and titles. These include working events such as Water and Draft Tests, which are described in another chapter. The club publishes manuals for training in these events and the standards for judging them. To earn a working title, a dog and handler must perform and pass certain exercises that demonstrate the dog's proficiency.

The NCA honors dogs and handlers who have completed multiple titles on their dogs with a Versatility Newfoundland (VN)

VN Ch. *Kilyka's* Deepwater and VN Ch. *Kilyka's* Benediction resting during a hike. These two ROM titled Newfs are among the top-producing dams and sires of the breed. Note the spotted tongue on the bitch (left). This is not at all unusual with Newfs. Bred and owned by Betty McDonnell. Photo by owner.

Constance Holt-Grenier bathing Ch. *Mooncusser's* Ships in the Night in preparation to compete at the National Specialty show. Dogs are both bathed and groomed at the show in order to look their very best in hope of prestigious wins. The dog is owned by his breeder, Sue Jones. Photo by Charisse Andrews.

title. To earn this title, dogs must have a Champion title in conformation, an obedience title, a Water Rescue Title, and a Draft Dog title.

Another coveted title awarded by NCA is the "Register of Merit" or ROM. The Register of Merit is awarded to dogs and bitches that have produced titled progeny with Champion, Obedience, and Working titles.

The club publishes a quarterly newsletter, Newf Tide, which contains articles on health, breeding, working activities and other educational material. The magazine serves to keep members up to date on board meetings, upcoming events, Newfs that have earned new titles, and the activities of members. Other club publications are available for those interested in training their Newfs for water, draft work, and backpacking.

Twenty-five regional clubs are sanctioned by the NCA. These clubs function autonomously under by-laws approved by the NCA. They have the same concerns as the parent club but also deal with regional interests. Members have the opportunity to meet, share problems and information, train their dogs, and enjoy activities on a regular basis. The parent club may approve regional clubs to host NCA Specialty shows and Water and Draft Tests.

The NCA is licensed by the AKC to hold Newfoundland Specialty shows. For Newf fanciers, the highlight of the year is the National Specialty show. This is usually a five-day event held in the spring. Each year the show is hosted by one of the regional clubs and is held in a different location.

Newfoundland fanciers from the fifty states and as far away as Europe and Australia have the opportunity to meet and watch the best Newfs compete in conformation, obedience, and sometimes, Water and Draft Tests. They come to show their dogs, visit with old friends, and meet members they may know by name but have never seen. They exchange ideas and information and have the opportunity to assess breeding programs of their own and of others. Besides the show itself, which is spread over four days, there are the Annual Meeting of the NCA, and seminars on health, breeding, working activities, and obedience. The event ends with a banquet.

Puppy Sweepstakes offer an opportunity for breeders to exhibit young Newfs under eighteen months of age, and Junior Showmanship classes assess the handling abilities of fanciers under eighteen years of age. Veteran Sweepstakes is an exhibition of Newfs older than age seven.

The first National Specialty was held in 1933 in conjunction with the Morris and Essex Kennel Club show in Madison, New Jersey. The first independently held National Specialty took place in Lenox, Massachusetts, in 1967. Since that date all but one or two National Specialties have been held independently. Entries have increased from 117 in 1967 to between 500 and 600 dogs at the more recent shows.

The increase in entries has paralleled the increase in breed registrations. Until the mid-1960s, the Newfoundland was a little-known breed. About that time there was a huge surge in interest in all purebred breeds.

Nashau-Auke's Snow in Summer staying cool under the tent while waiting her turn to be judged at the National Specialty. Summer is owned by her breeder, Jane Thibault. Photo by David Thibault.

A lineup of dogs during the final judging for Best of Breed at the National Specialty. Photo by Jeff Visotsky.

AKC individual registrations in all breeds rocketed from about 443,000 in 1960 to over 1,000,000 in 1970. Newfoundland registrations also began an upward swing. By 1970, there were 1,557 registrations. In 2001, there were 2,900 registrations.

Excessive popularity or becoming a "fad breed" is never desired by those concerned about the future of their breed. Popularity encourages indiscriminate breeding for commercial purposes. Since the early 1970s, the AKC registration ranking of Newfoundlands has maintained a comfortable position of around fiftieth among 148 AKC-recognized breeds. So far the Newfoundland has come into its own as a widely recognized and admired breed without facing the hazards of popularity.

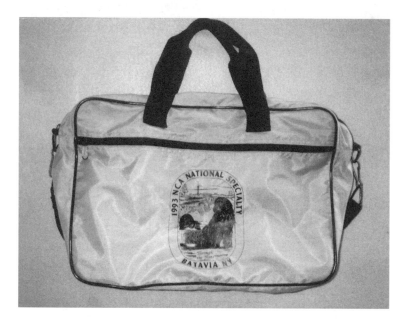

Mementos from National Specialty shows. Every year, each attendee receives a tote bag, a mug, and a pin, medallion, or key chain commemorating the event. Photos by author.

NEWFOUNDLANDS BEYOND OUR BORDERS

DIFFERENCES AND SIMILARITIES

11

LONG BEFORE THERE WAS ANY SCIENTIFIC knowledge of genetics, farmers, herders, and others involved with breeding animals for domestic use were aware that they could improve their stock by breeding to animals that produced certain desirable traits in their offspring. They looked for animals that could improve milk production in their goats, fleece on their sheep, or strength in their draft animals, and doubled up on favorable traits by inbreeding. They also learned that, from time to time, it was essential to breed to animals unrelated to their own stock in order to restore hybrid vigor.

Modern animal husbandry seeks for similar improvements, albeit with more sophistication and knowledge than the early agrarians

had. Knowledge of genetics and generations of written pedigrees, not to mention a wealth of computer data, all enhance the science of breeding better animals. These tools are used by today's dog breeders, as well as breeders of animals used for commercial purposes.

Newfoundland breeders worldwide seek to improve their stock by breeding to dogs whose traits they feel will complement and/or improve their own dogs. In addition to using their own males, they send their bitches to other breeders for stud services; purchase puppies or adults from other breeders; and may take a stud dog "on loan" to be used on a number of bitches before he is returned. The use of chilled or frozen semen has made it even easier to breed to a male some distance

Lineup of all the class winners at an Australian championship show. All the Newfs in this lineup are Dan Ruff's progeny. Photo by Enid Cummings.

away. These practices are carried on within and between countries, broadening the gene pool.

At one time there was more Newfoundland stock imported into the United States for breed improvement than was exported. Puppies and adults were purchased mostly from the Netherlands, England, and Denmark. By the 1970s, however, U.S. and Canadian stock became prized by breeders worldwide and the import-export balance changed. European breeders imported puppies and adults. Some American and Canadian stud dogs or brood bitches were sent abroad "on loan" to trusted breeders.

Breeders in the U.S. and Canada have been able to show, import dogs, and obtain stud services across the border with a minimum of government regulation. Most of the European countries have also been able to show, import, and export among themselves

Ch. *Topmast's* Fiddler, a Best in Show winner, shown here at nine years old. Owned by breeder and photographed by Ellen Stomp.

and North America. The exceptions have been the United Kingdom, Norway, Sweden, and Finland—all considered "rabies free" countries that have government-imposed quarantine systems. Because of the quarantine restrictions, these countries have been limited mostly to importing and exporting among themselves.

Quarantine means that a dog or puppy must be kept in a government-approved quarantine kennel for six months after arriving in the destination country. Breeders are understandably reluctant to sell dogs and puppies when they are forced to go through that system. It is especially hard on puppies, which need attention and socialization during the formative months. In addition, quarantine adds a considerable amount to the cost of an animal for the importing breeder.

Hawaii, Australia, and New Zealand also had quarantine restrictions. Previously, these two nations and Hawaii imported mostly from rabies-free Scandinavia and the United Kingdom. However, the restrictions have been eased considerably in all three of these areas. Australia, New Zealand, and Hawaii now require that dogs be quarantined for only thirty days assuming a number of strict conditions are met before shipping, making importation more practical.

The Scandinavian countries and the United Kingdom are easing restrictions as well. With dogs that meet required conditions, it now is possible to move dogs to or from most European countries for showing, breeding, selling, and stud services. Dogs sent directly from the United States and Canada must still go through a six-month quarantine in Scandinavia and Great Britain, or must have lived in another European country for that long.

The relatively recent interbreeding among North American and European Newfoundlands has resulted in less variation in style between the continents than what we saw fifteen or twenty years ago. Now at dog shows in Europe it is often difficult to guess whether a dog was bred in North America or in its home country. Breeders in

Left to right, Ch. *Topmast's* Hello Dolly, Ch. *Topmast's* Cotton Candy, and Can. Am. Ch. *Topmast's* Prairie Lily, all bred and owned by Marg Willmott of Saskatchewan. Photo by Gary Heisler.

Denmark and Italy led the way in importing and using dogs from North America, but American-style dogs can now be seen at shows in most countries. It is interesting to note that many European breeders give their dogs American names and some have even taken American kennel names.

The most obvious difference between the American-style dog and the older European style is in the head and body proportions. The American dog has a broader, shorter, and deeper muzzle, with the top of the skull more rounded than flat. American dogs tend to be slightly longer in body than the European-style dogs.

Some European breeders still prefer the style of dog that is more traditional in their country, so there are still a variety of types abroad. In Europe, the Landseer is bred, registered, and shown as a separate breed. However, white and black dogs from registered Newfoundland stock are shown throughout the continent as Newfoundlands.

Until the "iron curtain" came down, there was little opportunity to see what was being produced in Eastern Europe. Now their dogs can be shown in other countries, so it is possible to see some fine Newfs in former iron curtain countries.

Gross de la Linn o'Kokh with his owner's son, Dannie. "Grossie" is the son of a French dog, Skiff de la Pierre o'Kohn (belonging to one of the diplomats in the French embassy), that was bred to a local bitch in Kazan, Russia. He proudly wears some of approximately fifty medals won at dog shows. Grossie was owned by J. A. Tokmin; breeder unknown. Photo by Helen Tokmin.

AUSTRIA

Two Austrian swimmers: *Baerenkind* Adonis Aestivalis, owned by Peter Henhapl, and Air India *vom Schwarzen Baeren*, owned by Christine Buchner. Photo by Marina Froehlich.

At an Austrian search and rescue dog event, Ch. Obelix *vom Schwarzen Baeren* and Yeti *vom Schwarzen Baeren* take a rest from pulling their cart. Both dogs are owned by Marina and Arno Froehlich. Photo by owners.

DENMARK

CH *Bjornebanden's* Try For an Oscar on a shore in Denmark. Owned by breeders Winnie and Soren Wesseltoft. Photo by Soren Wesseltoft.

Ursula's National Express, bred and owned by Birgitta and Camilla Gothen and Folke Isaksson. Photo by Birgitta Gothen.

BELGIUM

Int'l, Italian, Austrian, Swedish, Norwegian Ch. *Twillin Gate* Quintex, bred in Belgium by Maria and Patrick Bogaerts, and owned by Manlio Massa of Italy. Photo by Paola Visintini.

HUNGARY

Multi-Champion, Multi-Best in Show *Midnight Lady's* Especially For You. This Hungarian dog was the top-producing sire in the United States in 2001. Bred by Zsuzsa Somos and Attila Soos. Owned by breeders and P. Helming, M. Massa, and B. Siklosi. Photo by breeders.

NORWAY

Norwegian, Swedish Ch. *Bikorella's* Oula, bred and owned by Astrid Indreboe and Knut Gjersem. Oula was the Gold Newfoundland bitch in Norway in 1999 and 2000. Photo by Astrid Indreboe.

ITALY

Multi-titled Ch. *Cayuga* What a Wonderful World of Bonaventura, bred and owned by Manlio Massa of Italy. Photo by Paola Visintini.

World, European, Int'l, American, Italian, Belgian, French, Swedish, Austrian, Norwegian, Finnish, Nordic, Italian Ch. *Cayuga* Ike Marshall of Bonaventura. According to his owner, he is the top championship titled Newfoundland in the history of the breed. Bred and owned by Manlio Massa. Photo by owner.

Ch. *Waterbear* Dan Ruff, bred and owned by Denise and Allen Robins. Dan had twenty-five Best in Show wins and five Specialty show wins in Australia. Nine of his progeny were also Best in Show winners. Photo by Christopher Shute.

For many years, the South Australian Canine Association commemorated the Best in Show winner for the year by bottling port wine and applying a custom label featuring the dog's picture. This is Dan Ruff's label. Photo by Chris Hill.

Japan was a latecomer to the sport of purebred dogs, but once they embraced the sport, they did it with zeal, importing stock in many breeds. Japan has a quarantine system, but it is not difficult to meet the requirements so that fanciers have been able to import dogs without heavy restrictions. Perhaps because of the compactness of Japanese cities and homes, large dogs such as Newfoundlands have not been in as much demand as smaller breeds. Israel is also a relative newcomer to Newfoundlands, but it has an active club and is working to improve the breed.

Showing dogs is as popular in Europe as in the United States. Instead of traveling from state to state for shows, European fanciers not only travel within their own borders, but from one country to another to show their dogs and gain championship titles. Dog shows are also popular in Australia and New Zealand. Clubs in both countries often share the costs of bringing in a judge from Europe, the United States, or Canada. By holding shows a week or so apart, the judge can perform in both countries.

Communication across the world has accelerated greatly. E-mail and faxes allow for fast, inexpensive communication, so that a breeder or fancier might exchange ideas and information as easily with someone a half-world away as with someone next door. Communication is enhanced when Newfoundland clubs invite judges from other countries to adjudicate their Specialty shows.

Fanciers and breeders from around the world are members of the Newfoundland

New Zealand's first brown champion, NZ Ch. *Karazan* Hot Chocolate (imp. U.K.), bred by Mr. and Mrs. J. Colgan and owned by Anne Rogers. Photo by L. Geldof.

Club of America and regularly attend the National Specialty show. Most European countries, as well as Australia and New Zealand, are represented each year. Some attendees bring dogs to compete at the Specialty, while others come to look or to purchase a dog. Judges from other countries are sometimes invited to judge at the show.

In 1996, the Italian Newfoundland Club held an "International Meeting of the Breed" in Turin, Italy. Speakers and attendees gathered from all parts of the Newfoundland world. Topics included health issues, breeding, color inheritance, and more. Instant translation was made possible by using headphones, so the audience could listen to the speakers in their own languages, much like at the United Nations. This was an outstanding endeavor to bring together fanciers worldwide and provide for the exchange of ideas.

Newf fanciers traveling in other countries can visit kennels and attend shows. Visitors are usually welcomed with cordiality and interest. It has become a small world.

Ch. *Gentle Bear* Royal Dane, bred and owned by Anne Rogers. Brown is a common Newf color in both New Zealand and Australia and many of their best Newfs are browns. Photo by Anne Rogers.

White and black puppies show variations in markings. The ones on the far left and the far right have white "blazes" on their heads. They were bred by Marg Willmott, whose *Topmast* Kennels in Saskatchewan are known for fine "Landseers." Photo by John Willmott.

BREEDING AND WHELPING

AN AWESOME RESPONSIBILITY

12

BREEDING IS BOTH AN ART AND A SCIENCE. It is a step that should be taken only after you have lived with, shown, and learned about Newfs. The only valid reason for becoming a breeder is the desire to perpetuate and enhance the best qualities of the breed—never just to produce more pets.

Being a breeder requires experience, study, and a broad knowledge of the breed. A breeder should be knowledgeable about genetic defects and their transmission, familiar with pedigrees and bloodlines, and able to recognize faults and determine whether a dog or bitch is of breeding quality.

Breeding is not for sissies. Raising a litter of puppies can be exhausting, as well as heartbreaking. It requires a significant cash outlay before the puppies are even whelped. Veterinary fees for prenatal care, stud fees, costs for shipping or transporting the bitch to the stud (sometimes with no resulting litter), long distance telephone charges, costs of constructing a whelping box and acquiring the necessary equipment (bedding, heat lamp, heating pad, and scales) are only the beginning. Whelping and post-partum veterinary costs are routinely incurred, even if no problems develop with the dam or the litter. The fee for a caesarean section, if needed, and veterinary care for sick puppies or a sick dam can make these costs skyrocket. Additional pens, food and feeding equipment, litter registration fees, worming, and puppy immunizations are all necessary expenses.

Today's more sophisticated buyers expect that the parents of the puppy they buy have been x-rayed for hip and elbow dysplasia, and that the puppies have been screened for heart defects, specifically, sub-aortic stenosis. It is preferable that a board certified cardiologist examine them. Having this done may require long drives with a litter to a large city clinic or veterinary school. It also means keeping all the puppies from nine to twelve weeks of age, or even longer if a suspect murmur is found in one or more puppies. While the murmur may prove to be "innocent," the breeder has the expense of feeding, caring for, and immunizing such puppies until they are cleared. All of this is a very expensive process.

Assuming all goes well with a normal-sized litter, the breeder might cover expenses when the puppies are sold. Even then, the costs may not be over. Most buyers expect the breeder to provide a guarantee of refund or replacement if their puppy is disabled by a hereditary defect. Funds should be set aside for the duration of the guarantee period to cover these expenses should they become necessary.

It is often difficult for a beginning breeder to sell puppies. Unsold pups held for several weeks or months require a considerable outlay in feeding, additional immunizations, and advertising costs. If the breeder has a small litter of only two or three pups, the costs of breeding and raising them will probably not be covered.

VN Ch. *Kilyka's* Every Amenity with puppy. Bred and owned by Betty McDonnell. Photo by Betty McDonnell.

It is never advisable to buy your first Newf with the idea of breeding. However, if you have been involved with the breed, or have raised other breeds for a while and you are sure that you already have a bitch of breeding quality, you may want to explore the option. Showing, membership in a regional Newfoundland club and/or an all-breed club, and association with other Newf fanciers can help provide knowledge and experience for the prospective breeder. Fellow fanciers often are eager to assist new breeders who are sincerely interested in improving and preserving the breed

THE BROOD BITCH

The breeding life of a Newfoundland bitch begins when she comes into season for the first time at the age of ten to sixteen months. Thereafter, she will come in season at roughly six-month intervals. Fertility increases from puberty to full maturity and then declines until a state of total sterility is reached in old age. It is not considered ethical to breed a bitch during her first estrus, nor before she is close to two years of age. The bitch needs to mature both physically and emotionally before having a litter.

Two or three months before a bitch is to be mated, her physical condition should be considered carefully. If she is too thin, provide a rich, balanced diet plus the regular exercise needed to develop strong, supple muscles. An overweight bitch will need even more exercise and a reduction of food to bring her into optimum condition. About a month before her season is due, a prospective brood bitch should be given booster shots and a veterinarian should examine a stool specimen for worms. If there is evidence of infestation, the bitch should be wormed.

The length of the heat cycle varies from eighteen to twenty-one days. The first indication is a pronounced swelling of the vulva with coincidental bleeding (called "showing color") for about the first seven to nine days. The discharge gradually turns to a creamy color, and it is during this phase (estrus), from about the tenth to fifteenth day, that the bitch is ovulating and receptive to the male. Since many Newf bitches continue to show color through the

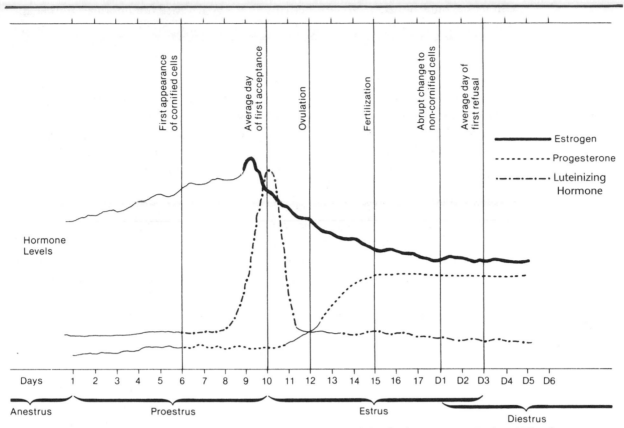

The estrous cycle in the bitch. Note how the LH peak triggers ovulation and that fertilization occurs in the middle of estrus, approximately five days after a bitch will first accept.

receptive period, color alone should not be used to determine when a bitch is ready to be bred. The ripe, unfertilized ova survive for about seventy-two hours after ovulation. If fertilization doesn't occur, the ova die and are discharged. If fertilization does take place, each ovum attaches itself to the wall of the uterus. A membrane forms to seal off the ovum, and it develops into an embryo.

Following the estrus phase, the bitch is still in season until about the twenty-first day and will continue to attract males, although she will usually fight them off as she did the first few days. Nevertheless, to avoid accidental mating, the bitch must be confined for the entire period. Virtual imprisonment is necessary, for male dogs display uncanny abilities in their efforts to reach a bitch in season.

THE STUD DOG

Your search for a suitable mate for your bitch should begin long before she is due to come in season, and arrangements need to be made well in advance. It is beyond the scope of this book to discuss all the factors involved in selecting a male. You should consult some of the excellent books available on breeding theory and genetics (see Other Sources of Information). Look for a male that is a superior specimen of the breed that also cross-faults well with your bitch. The owner of the stud should provide a stud service contract. Stud fees and the date they are payable should be negotiated in advance.

A dog can be used at stud from the time he reaches physical maturity well into old age. For the safety of the stud dog, at least one experienced person should assist with breeding.

Bitches should be securely held, perhaps muzzled, to prevent injury from a bitch biting out of fear or pain. Furthermore, a bitch may need to be supported to prevent injury to the stud from any attempt to sit or pull away during a breeding. Without this support, a bitch can be overpowered by a stud dog's weight. She might also attempt to escape because of pain or excitement.

If a stud dog owner accepts a bitch for breeding, he should make every attempt to get natural breedings. It is general practice to breed a bitch twice, skipping a day between breedings. If the bitch is still receptive, a third breeding may be attempted in another forty-eight hours. Usually the mating will be successful. As a last resort, artificial insemination can be accomplished by a veterinarian. Artificial insemination can be just as successful as a natural breeding.

However, if it is not, an additional service may be given free of charge, provided the stud dog is still in the possession of the same owner. If the bitch misses, it may be because her cycle varied from normal. You veterinarian can use several methods to determine when the bitch is entering the estrus phase and when ovulation is most likely to occur.

The litter registration application is completed only after the puppies are whelped, and it must be signed by the owner of the stud as well as the owner of the bitch. Registration forms may be secured from the American Kennel Club.

PREGNANCY

The gestation period normally lasts nine weeks, although it may vary from sixty-one to sixty-five days. If it goes beyond sixty-five days from the date of mating, consult a veterinarian.

In a normal pregnancy, there is visible enlargement of the abdomen by the end of the fifth week. Using palpation (feeling with the fingers), ultrasound, or x-ray, a veterinarian may be able to distinguish developing

Left, Ch. *Amity's* Bearfoot of *Pouch Cove*, ROM, was top sire in 1987 and 1989. He was bred by Diane Broderick and Peggy Helming and owned by Peggy and David Helming. Right, CH *Pouch Cove* Gref of Newton, AR, ROM, was bred by Peggy Helming and Janet Levine. He was owned by Julie Heyward. Gref is the sire of Bearfoot. Both were very prominent sires. Photo by Ashbey Photography.

puppies as early as three weeks after mating, but it is unwise for a novice to poke and prod to try to detect the presence of unborn puppies.

During the first four or five weeks of pregnancy, the bitch should be permitted her normal amount of activity. As she becomes heavier, she should be walked on leash. Strenuous running and jumping should be avoided. Her diet should be increased after it is known she is in whelp, and feeding can be divided into several small meals per day as she approaches her whelping date.

A whelping box should be secured about two weeks before the puppies are due, and the bitch should be accustomed to sleeping in it by the time the puppies arrive. The box should be approximately four by six feet in size, with a "ledge" or rail around the top that will confine small puppies and provide a sheltered nook to prevent them from being crushed or smothered by the dam.

BIRTH OF THE LITTER

Forty-eight to seventy-two hours before whelping, you will probably note a definite change in the shape of the abdomen. As the time becomes imminent, the bitch will scratch and root at her bedding in an effort to make a nest, and may refuse food and ask to be let out every few minutes. However, the surest sign is a drop in her temperature to ninety-nine degrees or lower about twelve hours before labor begins. The bitch will sit and pant. When hard labor actually begins, the bitch's abdomen and flanks will contract sharply as she attempts to expel a puppy, then she will rest for a while and try again. Someone should stay with the bitch the entire time that whelping is taking place, and if she appears to be having unusual difficulties a veterinarian should be called.

Puppies usually are born head first, though some may be born feet first with no difficulty. Each puppy is enclosed in a separate membranous sac that the bitch will remove with her teeth, although sometimes the sac breaks and the fluid in it is expelled with the pup. If the bitch does not break the sac the breeder should do so, so the puppy can start breathing. The dam will sever the umbilical cord attached to the soft, spongy afterbirth that is expelled right after the puppy emerges. If necessary, the breeder can cut the cord with a dull, but sterile, scissors

Dam and her puppies in the whelping box. Note the "ledge" around the top of the box. If a puppy crawls behind the dam, the ledge prevents her from rolling backward onto the pup. Drawing by Alan Riley.

A NORMAL BIRTH

A normal birth; the puppy is head first. Note the way the birth canal curves over the pelvic bone. If you need to assist, always pull down, and forward, towards the bitch's stomach.

A BREECH BIRTH

The puppy's rear is first. Breech births are sometimes more difficult. If possible, keep the bitch from breaking the sac until the puppy's head is out.

after pushing any blood toward the puppy's body first. If the cord bleeds, it can be tied off with thread or dental floss about a half inch from the puppy's body.

Usually the bitch will attempt to eat the afterbirth. Make sure an afterbirth is expelled for each puppy whelped. If an afterbirth is retained, the bitch could develop pyometra (a uterine infection) and die, so if you think an afterbirth has been retained you must have a veterinarian check the bitch within no more than twelve or fourteen hours after whelping.

It is imperative to get the new puppy breathing. You will know it is breathing when it lets out a cry. If the bitch is not at-

tempting to clean her puppy, and sometimes maternal instincts are delayed with first litters, take the newborn and give it a brisk rubdown with a heavy towel, holding the puppy's head down so that any fluids can drain from the throat. Time is critical and breathing must not be delayed. If initial efforts fail, take the skin on the nape of the neck and, rotating your wrist, twist left and right and repeat until you get a cry of life. Another way to stimulate breathing is to put a few drops of brandy on the whelp's tongue. A last resort effort is to blow gently into the pup's mouth or nose to inflate his lungs. Many a "stillborn" has been revived by persistence.

The newborn should be eager to nurse immediately. It is important that each pup get some of the bitch's colostrum, or first milk, for it provides necessary early immunity. You can assist any pups that are not nursing by squeezing some milk to the surface of the teat and then opening the pup's mouth to insert the teat. Hold the pup in place until he is actively sucking.

When the bitch is ready to expel another whelp, place those puppies born earlier in a box lined with clean towels and warmed by a heat lamp from above or a heating pad inside the box. Check the box frequently to be sure it is not too hot. Puppies are unable to regulate their own temperatures for the first week or so, and they must not be allowed to overheat or chill. Whelping sometimes continues for as long as twenty-four hours for a very large litter, but a litter of two or three puppies may be whelped in a few hours. The bitch periodically should be offered cool, fresh water. If the whelping continues over a period of several hours, she may be offered small amounts of food to help keep up her strength. When the bitch settles down and is content to sleep with her litter, this usually indicates that all the puppies have been delivered. (The average number of puppies in an Newfoundland litter is eight.)

Within twelve hours after whelping, the bitch should be taken to the vet, who will determine if she has retained any puppies. The vet will probably give her a shot of oxytocin to help her uterus to contract and expel any retained afterbirth.

Puppies should be weighed at birth and every day for the first week. After that, continue twice-weekly weighing until four weeks, then weekly weighing is sufficient. Weights should be recorded so you can see if any puppy is failing to thrive. The chart makes an interesting comparison for later litters.

Because most Newf litters are similar in color and size, you will need to identify each pup for weighing, for administering medications, and for whatever "treatments" such as worming and vaccination are needed. Especially with an all-black litter, it is almost impossible to know who is who without easy-to-see identification. Some breeders use very thick, soft yarn in a variety of colors tied around the puppies' necks. Of course, these "collars" need to be checked and replaced as the pups grow or as they become worn. You can tell each puppy at a glance by the color of his collar. Other breeders use one family of colors, reds, for example, for female puppies and blues for males. There are times when you want to easily tell males from females.

During the first weeks after delivery, the bitch's temperature should be checked daily, and any dramatic elevation should be reported to the veterinarian. She will have a vaginal discharge for a few weeks and this should be checked to make sure there is no evidence of infection. Her breasts must be palpated daily to check for mastitis, an udder infection which is painful to the bitch and may poison the puppies. The bitch's breasts and vulva should be rinsed daily to keep them clean and to keep down the odor from the vaginal discharge. The whelping box should have clean padding for sanitation. Blankets, old quilted bedspreads, or any other fabric with good absorbency and traction may be used to line the box. You should have enough on hand to change bedding as needed while the soiled bedding is being washed and dried.

For weak or very small puppies, supplemental feeding is often recommended. One method is to use a standard baby bottle and preemie nipple; another is tube-feeding with a catheter attached to a syringe. An experienced person should demonstrate this latter method. Do not use cow's milk. Commercially prepared puppy formulas resembling bitch's milk are convenient and are readily obtainable from a veterinarian or pet supply store.

WEANING

Supplemental feeding for all the puppies should begin when they are about three weeks of age. The amount fed each day should be increased over a period of three weeks, until the puppies are weaned completely. Start hand-feeding each puppy individually. A recommended starter supplement would be pureed baby meat, about the size of a golf ball, with water added so that pups can suck it off your fingers. This can be given as early as two weeks of age if necessary. (Raw hamburger is no longer advised because of the danger of E. coli.)

Puppy kibble that is soaked to a mush in hot water may be used for the first "bowl" feeding at three weeks. You can include some milk formula, pureed baby meat, or a bit of premium canned dog food, all mixed together in a blender. The puppies can eat from a communal pan, but be sure that the small ones get their share. If they are pushed aside, feed them separately. Gradually increase the number of meals and cut back on the time the dam is allowed with her puppies. When the puppies are about six weeks old, they should be weaned completely. Four meals a day are sufficient from this time until the puppies are about ten weeks old, when feeding can be reduced to three meals a day, then twice a day at six months. Ideally, this schedule should be followed for the rest of the dog's life.

Puppies need to be moved to larger quarters at around three weeks. Until they

These babies are old enough to leave the confines of a pen and explore a bit. Bred at the *Ursula* Kennels in Denmark. Photo by Camilla Gothen.

A litter of hungry puppies feeding at the *Bjornebanden* Kennels in Denmark. Each pup has his own "station" to make sure the greedy ones don't get more than their share. Photo by Soren Wesseltoft.

begin to eat solid food, the dam will eat their feces. Once on solid food, the whelping box quickly becomes fouled. At six weeks the pups can be moved to outdoor quarters with plenty of room to play and exercise. A dry, heated shelter is necessary in cold weather. Shelter from rain and sun is needed in warm weather. Safe, secure fencing is a must.

Once they are weaned, the puppies should be given their first vaccinations, which need to be repeated according to your vet's recommendations. At three weeks, stool specimens should be checked for worms. Specimens should be checked again at five weeks, and as often thereafter as your veterinarian recommends.

As mentioned earlier, Newfs may be born with heart defects that can result in premature death as early as a few months of age. Puppies' hearts should be checked beginning at six weeks, and then several times afterward by a veterinary cardiologist, or, at the least, by a veterinarian who has learned to diagnose sub-aortic stenosis. Puppies with suspicious murmurs should not be placed in new homes until, or unless, these murmurs "clear" at a later age.

PLACING THE PUPPIES

Unless you plan to keep a pup to continue a breeding program, there is no point in breeding. When the time comes to place the puppies, you will want to keep the best one or ones for yourself. If you need help in selecting which puppy to keep, enlist the help of an experienced breeder. You should make this decision before offering the other puppies for sale.

Be prepared to screen prospective buyers to ascertain that they will make suitable owners for your precious puppies. You have the right to turn down anyone for whom you have unfavorable "vibes" or for any other reason, such as work schedules, lack of fencing, or whatever. If selling to a family, it is wise to have the children come with the parents to see the puppies so you can sense whether they are capable of treating a puppy with respect. You don't want to see anyone walk away with one of your pups if you have reservations about them. You may want to give "limited registrations" on puppies unless the owners are willing to show them, or until the pups have been neutered. Any agreements you have with the owners must be in writing. When the pups are ready to leave, you should have prepared and ready for the new owners: a sales contract, a list of worming and vaccinations that the puppies have already had, health and heart check documentation from your veterinarian, and a recommended feeding schedule showing what food the puppies have been fed. You will have registered the litter with the AKC and have the individual registration slips ready to give the buyers when they take their puppies.

All of the above is but an overview on breeding. The best advice and help you can get is through the breeder from whom you bought your bitch and through fellow regional Newfoundland

A brown puppy bred and owned by Anne Rogers of New Zealand. Photo by owner.

This *Shadrack* puppy appears to be gray, but he is really black. Black Newfs are tricky to photograph. Lighting and camera settings can make black dogs appear gray or brown. Detail may be lost unless the photo is a little overexposed. Photo by Jan Boggio.

club members who are experienced Newfoundland breeders. They can assist you with advice on local resources needed in whelping and caring for a litter and in registering the litter, screening buyers, writing contracts and so on. If there are no Newfoundland breeders in your area, any reputable breeder of a large or giant breed can be of help. You will probably have met some of these people while showing and training your bitch. The dog world has many helpful people who are anxious to pass on their knowledge. There is no reason to try to "go it alone" in something as serious as breeding, raising a litter, and selling the puppies.

Ch. *Birkorella's* Vinebird Tiki, owned and photographed by Astrid Indreboe, Norway.

YOUR OLDER NEWFOUNDLAND

PREPARING TO SAY FAREWELL

13

As your Newfoundland ages, you will find his muzzle graying and his steps becoming slower. He may sleep for more of the day. The average lifespan of a Newfoundland is only about ten years. The older dog is subject to a number of medical problems including hypothyroidism, cataracts, and degenerative joint diseases. After the age of six it becomes especially important to have regular annual physical and dental checkups done on your Newf. Regular teeth cleaning and care of diseased teeth or gums can help prevent heart disease and infections. Blood tests can detect a lowering of the dog's thyroid levels or a tendency toward kidney or liver problems. With proper care your dog can be healthy and active into his later years.

Your older dog will need a warm, draft-free environment in winter and a cool place in the summer. He should have plenty of clean water available at all times. Find a diet that works and stay with it; no table scraps, sudden changes, or continuing variety. The older dog generally does best on a diet that is not too high in either protein or fat. Senior formulas are produced by nearly all of the premium food manufacturers.

Keep abreast of new research published on the Newfoundland Club of America website and also from your local veterinarian. We are learning more each year about supplements and treatments for joint and bone problems, as well as other diseases. New research on diets for dogs appears regularly in publications. As we strive to live longer, healthier, human lives, veterinarians are working toward the same goal for our pets.

PREPARING FOR THE INEVITABLE

Dogs worm their way into our hearts and lives to become beloved members of our families. However, they do not live long enough. Foreseeing death is one of the curses of being human. No one who loves a dog fails to recognize that great sadness lies ahead when the dog dies. Many of us try to protect ourselves from the loneliness that losing a dog entails by having several dogs, so that another will be there when the inevitable happens to one beloved pet. It does help, to some extent, but each dog is such an individual that there is still a gaping hole.

One way to prepare is to keep the memories alive with plenty of mementos of your dog's life. A scrapbook of photographs, a footprint, a sample of his hair coat or a favorite collar, and a list of favorite people, toys, and activities is a nice way of preserving memories. Remember to take videos during your dog's puppyhood and of any activities or competitions. You may collect an array of ribbons, certificates, and other awards. Display them with your favorite photos. After your pet is gone, you will be so glad to have these memories.

BY THE KITCHEN DOOR

There's an empty place by the kitchen door,
The place where Jake used to lay.
It's empty now and forever more,
...Jake has gone away.

No more will we watch him run up the hill,
With his beautiful head held high.
We just weren't ready for him to go,
Weren't ready to say good-bye.

It seems that even the cattle and deer,
With whom he would run and play,
Know that their big black friend's not here,
Know that he's gone away.

My heart is sad as I mourn my friend,
Who was loving and loyal and true.
As I look at the empty spot by the door,
I wonder what I will do.

Then I feel a nudge under my arm,
And a wet tongue licks my face.
I look down at a face so familiar to me
That my sadness seems out of place.

The empty place by the kitchen door,
Will never be empty, I see,
For Jake, I now know, will always be there.
He has left us his legacy.

Rachel and Mathew, Hunter and Skip
And many, many more.
Jake's spirit lives on and can always be found,
In his place by the kitchen door.

Debby Summers

Ch. *Pouch Cove's* Favorite Son, "Jake," who was honored by Debby Summers' poem. Jake is the all-time top-producing sire in the breed and was influential in both the U.S. and Europe. He was a multiple Best in Show winner and the Best of Breed winner at the 1991 National Specialty. Above all, he was a dog widely admired and loved for himself. Jake was bred and owned by Peggy and David Helming. Painting by Alana Shirley. Photo by Peggy Helming.

Your dog will generally tell you when his time is coming. He begins to lose interest in food or exercise, or he develops an incurable medical condition. When this happens, the humane approach is to have him euthanized, or humanely "put to sleep" by your veterinarian.

Many communities have mobile vet services that will do this in your home so the dog experiences no stress or fear. You can choose to bury him on your own property (if the law allows) or in a pet cemetery, or you can have his body cremated.

Difficult as it may be, stay with your dear friend, hold and talk to him while he is eased out of the world by the veterinarian. Euthanasia is the final gift you can give your dog when it becomes necessary for the comfort of his body and spirit.

Dryad's Dark Star, ROM and holder of Obedience and Draft titles, is shown here at age thirteen and a half years, a ripe old age for a Newf. Owners are Joan Gunn and Alexandra Zemanek. Photo by Joan Gunn.

MOURNING THE LOSS

Today, it is recognized that mourning a lost pet is normal, even to the extent that there are support groups for people who need them. Not everyone will understand your grief, but anyone who has lost a pet knows the sense of emptiness the loss brings.

The death of a pet can be a profound experience for children. It may be their first experience with loss of a loved one. It is an opportunity for parents to show that grief is natural and that tears and talking about the pet are helpful. It can help children learn that they will remember their pets with affection, but that the intense grief will not last forever. It is important not to comfort a child by telling him or her that you will get another puppy, in a way that suggests that a new dog can replace a former pet. Make it clear that the family loved the old dog so much that they will want another dog when everyone feels ready,

while reminding them that the new dog will be different. Whether a human or a pet, children need to understand that no individual can be "replaced."

Poetry is a way some people express grief. Following are a few poems written by Newfoundland owners after the loss of a dog.

FOREVER SAFE

Pain binds my soul as I stumble
Through a frozen forest of tears
Guided only by the whimper of
the wind
Searching for what
was lost but waits to be found
Then darkness turned soft as silk
and warm as the sun with a
nudge of his nose I open my
eyes to find what I thought lost a
place in my heart to forever keep
him safe.

Larry E. Hansen Jr.

NEWF

You, old warrior,
Your days of labor over,
Sleep across hours,
Once, we, armed with no danger,
Sounding trumpets of sunlight,
Explored new worlds together.

Alan Riley

Lord Byron, the English poet, immortalized his beloved Newfoundland, Boatswain, in the following eulogy, a most moving tribute to the character of a Newfoundland:

Near this Spot
are deposited the Remains of one
who possessed Beauty without Vanity,
Strength without Insolence,
Courage without Ferocity,
and all the Virtues of Man without his
    Vices.
This praise, which would be unmeaning
    Flattery
if inscribed over human Ashes,
is but a just tribute to the Memory of
BOATSWAIN, a DOG,
who was born in Newfoundland May 1803
and died at Newstead Nov. 18th, 1808

Kim Spackman takes her parents' *Pouch Cove* Newfs for an autumn walk. Photo by Mary Jane Spackman.

APPENDIX A

LIST OF KENNELS REPRESENTED

KENNEL NAME	BREEDER-OWNER(S)	COUNTRY
Amity	Diane and Tom Broderick	U.S.
Baerenkind	Traude and Heinz Juan	Austria
Bearbrook	Hilda Deslauriers-Gintner	U.S.
Bearcove	Elizabeth and Gordon Barnett	New Zealand
Birkorella	Astrid Indrebo and Knut Gjersem	Norway
Bjornebanden	Winnie and Soren Wesseltoft	Denmark
Blackwatch	Joan Gunn	U.S.
Cameroon	Gloria Fundak and R. C. Harrison	U.S.
CastaNewf	Denise and Marc Castonguay	Canada
Cayuga	Manlio Massa	Italy
Cedar Pond	Kelly and Gus Economides	U.S.
Copperidge	Elizabeth Stiles	U.S.
Cypress Bay	Debra and Marvin Thornton	U.S.
Darbydale	Carol Bergmann	U.S.
Dorlin	Doreen Linkletter	Canada
Dryad	Mary Dewey	U.S.
Gentle Bear	Anne Rogers	New Zealand
Hickory Ridge	Kathy Smith	U.S.
Ironwood	Vicky and Larry Hansen	U.S.
Karazan	Mr. and Mrs. J. Colgan	U.K.
Kilyka	Betty McDonnell	U.S.
Kiredor	Linda and Stacy Roderick	U.S.
Midnight Lady	Zsuzsa Somos and Attila Soos	Hungary
Midnite Bay	Reggie Schneider	U.S.
Mooncusser	Sue Jones	U.S.
Nakiska	Ingrid and Chris Lyden	U.S.
Nashau-Auke	Jane Thibault	U.S.
Newton Ark	Janet and Allen Levine	U.S.
Numa	Diane Keyser	U.S.
Pooh Bear	Shelby Guelich	U.S.
Pouch Cove	Peggy and David Helming	U.S.
Seabrook	Kathy Griffin and Lou Lomax	U.S.
Seamount	JoAnn and Alan Riley	U.S.
Shadrack	Jean and Steve McAdams	U.S.
Sweetbay	Judi and Ellis Adler	U.S.
Tatoosh	Maree Lerchen	U.S.
Topmast	Marg and John Willmott	Canada
Twillin Gate	Maria and Patrick Bogaerts	Belgium
Ursula	Birgitta Gothen	Denmark
vom Schwarzen Baeren	Eva Obojes	Austria
Waterbear	Denise and Allan Robins	Australia

ORGANIZATIONS

The American Kennel Club
www.akc.org
AKC Operations Center
5580 Centerview Drive, Raleigh, NC 27606
(919) 233-9767
AKC Headquarters
260 Madison Ave, New York, NY 10016
(212) 696-8200

Newfoundland Club of America
www.newfdogclub.org

Newfoundland Rescue Network
(Maintains a list of local rescue contacts)
listed on www.newfdogclub.org

United Kennel Club
www.ukcdogs.com
100 E. Kilgore Rd.
Kalamazoo, MI 49002-5584
(269) 343-9020

The Canadian Kennel Club
http://www.ckc.ca
89 Skyway Avenue Suite 100
Etobicoke, Ontario
M9W 6R4

The Newfoundland Club of Canada
http://home.golden.net/~blacknita/
Offers links to many Newf clubs worldwide

Federation Cynologique Internationale
(the international dog show association)
http://www.fci.be
Place Albert 1er, 13
B-6530 Thuin
Belgium

The Kennel Club (Great Britian)
www.the-kennel-club.org.uk

Orthopedic Foundation for Animals
http://www.offa.org
2300 E. Nifong Boulevard
Columbia, MO 65201-3856

Canine Eye Registry Foundation
www.vet.purdue.edu/~yshen/cerf.html
CERF/Lynn Hall
625 Harrison St.
W. Lafayette, IN 47907-2026

Therapy Dogs, Inc.
www.therapydogs.com
P.O. Box 5868
Cheyenne, WY 82003

Therapy Dogs International
www.tdi-dog.org
88 Bartley Road
Flanders, NJ 07836

North American Dog Agility Council, Inc.
www.nadac.com
11522 South Hwy 3
Cataldo, ID 83810

United States Dog Agility Association, Inc.
http://www.usdaa.com
P.O. Box 850955
Richardson, TX 75085-0955

MAGAZINES

Newf Tide
Published by the Newfoundland Club of America
(see website listed above)

General Interest

AKC Gazette (show dogs)
AKC Family Dog (companion dogs)
www.akc.org/pubs/
260 Madison Avenue
New York, NY 10016

Dog World
www.dogworld.com
P.O. Box 56244
Boulder, CO 80322-6244

Dog Fancy
www.dogfancy.com
P.O. Box 53264
Boulder, CO 80322-3264

Performance Events

Off Lead Magazine (obedience)
www.off-lead.com
Barkleigh Productions, Inc.
6 State Road #113
Mechanicsburg PA 17050

Front and Finish (obedience)
www.frontandfinish.com
P.O. Box 333
Galesburg, IL, 61402

Clean Run (agility)
 www.cleanrun.com
35 North Chicopee Street †
Chicopee, MA 01020

Agility Trials
Clean Run Events Listings
www.cleanrun.com/agilityinfo/event

Draft Dog and Water Dog Trials
Newfoundland Club of America
www.newfdogclub.org

BOOKS

How to Raise a Puppy You Can Live With
Rutherford and Neil
Alpine Publications

Canine Reproduction: The Breeders Guide
Phyllis A. Holst, DVM
Alpine Publications

Clicking With Your Dog
Peggy Tillman
Sunshine Books

Click to Win: Clicker Training for the Show Ring
Karen Pryor
Sunshine Books

The New Dogsteps
Rachel Paige Elliot
Doral Publishing

Genetics for Dog Breeders
Jackie Isabell
Alpine Publications

Purely Positive Training
Sheila Booth
Podium Publications

Peak Performance: Coaching the Canine Athlete
Jumping From A to Z
M. Christine Zink DVM
Canine Sports Publications

The Dynamics of Canine Gait
Leon Hollenbeck
Denlinger Books

VIDEOS

Your Athletic Dog: A Functional Approach
Motivational Agility Training
www.flyingdogpress.com
Suzanne Clothier

Dogsteps
Rachel Page Elliot

Referrals to Trainers

National Association of Dog Obedience Instructors
www.nadoi.org

Clicker Trainers
http://clickerteachers.travelvan.net/mainpage.php

Dog Show Superintendents

Jack Bradshaw Dog Shows
www.jbradshaw.com

Roy Jones Dog Shows
http://www.royjonesdogshows.com

MB-F Inc.
http://www.infodog.com

McNulty Dog Shows
http://www.mcnultydogshows.com

Jack Onofrio Dog Shows
www.onofrio.com

Bob Peters Dog Shows
www.bpds.com

Rau Dog Shows
www.raudogshows.com

Kevin Rogers Dog Shows
www.rogersdogshows.com